Google

The Google Way:

How to Use Google to Do Everything!

By Hunter Travis

Minute Help Press

© 2011

Table of Contents

Introduction: A Brief History of Google

Google is a search engine and a suite of cloud-based web applications, including email, calendars, contacts, a web browser (Google Chrome), web docs, and more. Google's stated mission is to "organize the world's information and make it universally accessible and useful." The company's unofficial motto is "Don't be evil."

Google began its life as a web crawler created by two doctoral students at Stanford University in 1996. The students, Larry Page and Sergey Brin, were working on a dissertation project to effectively rank search engine results. At the time, search engines ranked results based on the number of times a keyword appeared on the page. This method was not effective, however, as keyword hits did not always accurately reflect a web page's relative importance.

To fix this problem, Page and Brin created Google, which looked at the backlinks between different websites and analyzed the data based on an algorithm. Page and Brin believed that the more backlinks that existed between a page and other relevant pages, then the more relevant and important the pages must be. The research proved Page and Brin were correct, as their model generated far more accurate and relevant results than the traditional 'keyword search' model.

Page and Brin officially registered Google.com in 1997 and created Google Inc. in 1998. The name itself is a nod to 'googol,' a term for the number one followed by 100 zeros. By December 1998, Google had an index of over 60 million pages. While the website itself was still in its 'Beta' stages, Google.com quickly gained a popular following as everyone from tech geeks to the mainstream media praised its clean design, user-friendly interface and superior search engine results.

Since Page and Brin's early days working out of a friend's garage at Stanford, Google has grown significantly. Today Google is a multinational public corporation that focuses on Internet searching, cloud computing, and advertising technologies. Google makes the majority of its profit from Google AdWords advertising. Google has signed lucrative partnerships with a number of major corporations and NASA to develop new technologies. The verb 'to google' is part of popular culture, as everyone from blind dates to prospective employers 'google' one another.

While you don't need an account to use Google as a search engine, you will need a

Google account to access Gmail and other cloud-based applications. If you don't already have one, setting up a Google account is free and quick. Get started by visiting www.google.com to sign up.

Chapter 1: Google Searching

Google redefined how we search the Internet. In the pre-Google days, search engines such as Lycos, Yahoo! and HotBot simply browsed pages for keyword hits. The greater the number of keyword hits, the higher the page ranked in the search results. This led to wide range of results from the very useful to the completely worthless. Google's search algorithm, which is based on back links between different pages, changed this, generating accurate and precise results. Today, Google is the world's most popular search engine and a powerful tool for finding information.

1.1 Getting started with Google Search.

To get started, go to Google.com. You'll be greeted with a simple page for entering your search term that looks like this:

Type in your search term and hit 'Enter.' For example, let's say you search for 'iPhone.' Your search results will look something like the image below. You'll see websites, news results and shopping results all in one place. Immediately below the search field is a paid ad; you may also see text ads in the right column.

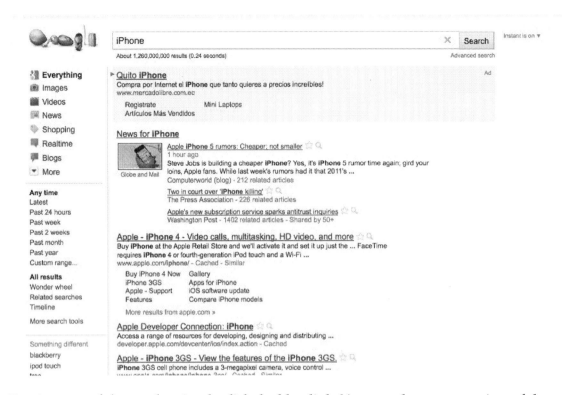

To view any of the results, simply click the blue link. You can also see a preview of the page by holding your mouse over the result or by clicking the magnifying glass to the right of the result.

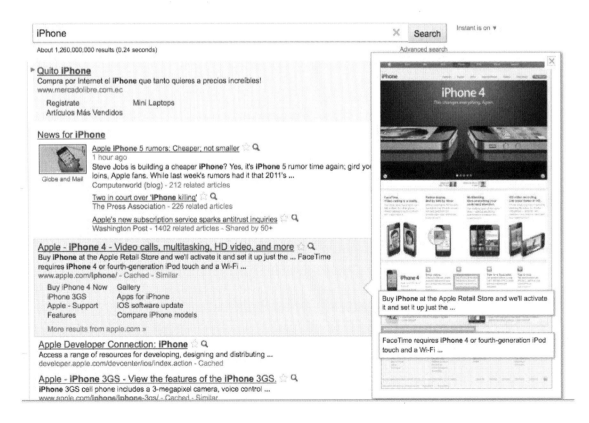

The order of the search results you see is based partially on Google's PageRank algorithm. Over the years, Google has also added other criteria to its algorithm to ensure that the search results closely correlate with the human concept of importance. Google indexes not only web pages, but also files, including PDF, Word documents, Excel spreadsheets, Flash SWF and image files.

Google's search engine accepts your query as simple text, breaking this text up into a sequence of key terms. For example, if you search 'where can I buy an iPhone 4 in California?' Google will break this phrase down into searchable terms based on location (California), need (buying an iPhone 4) and product (iPhone 4). If you misspell a word, Google will automatically correct it for you in the search results.

1.2 Advanced searches

Powering up your search with Boolean operators. Google also uses Boolean operators to find specific information. A list of common operators is below.

Operator	Definition	Example
""	Search as specific phrase exactly as entered	"President Barack Obama" will exclude results that only include "Barack Obama"
site:	Search within a specific site	Barack Obama site:nytimes.com
- (hyphen)	Exclude terms	Cowboys –Dallas (don't return results for the football team)
* (wildcard or fill in the blank)	Google will fill in the blank for you	Obama voted * on * bill
+ or """" (double quotes)	Search a term exactly as it is, do not use synonyms	""child care"" (no results with childcare as one word)

OR	Either option, result does not have to include both	Dallas Cowboys 2009 OR 2010

Search for specific content. You can select the type of content you wish to search using either the menu on the left of the search results or the top tool bar.

For example, to find only photos of iPhones, click the 'images' button from the tool bar or the left bar and only images will be displayed in your results.

1.3 Search history and settings

You can store your Google search history in your browser, Google toolbar or Google web history. In the Firefox web browser, click 'Manage Search Engines.' You'll see the following menu. Make sure the 'suggest searches as you type' checkbox is selected. Then when you start typing in a term, you'll see a list below of previous searches you've done with the term and suggested searches.

To save your Google searches in web history, you will first need to enable web history at google.com/history. Sign in to your Google account while searching. If you're signed in, the email address associated with your account will appear in the top right corner of the page.

1.4 Google Instant

Google Instant is a Google search function that instantly displays results as you type a term or phrase into the search field. As you continue to type, the results will dynamically update. Google Instant still uses the same algorithms to generate your search results. What has changed is the ability to now get to the results you want faster, as Google Instant predicts your queries. Take the iPhone search example we used earlier. If we just type in 'i' the following results are displayed. Based on our previous searches and the searches done by others, Google first guesses we are typing itunes, ikea, imdb, etc

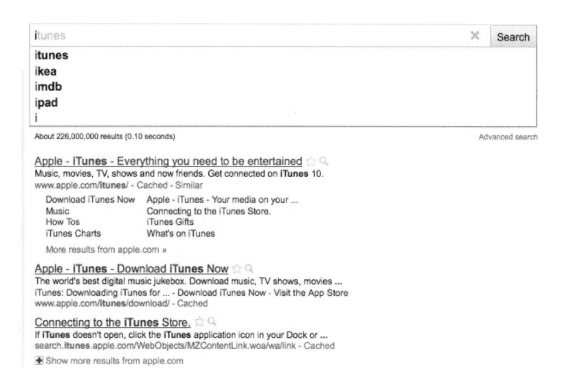

If we continue to type 'iPh', the top results are now all iPhone. We can stop typing and let Google Instant autofill our search term and click on the results below.

Google Instant makes searching faster, helping you get to the information you need efficiently and effectively. It also helps you search smarter. If as you type you don't see the search results you need, you can instantly refine your search by adding additional terms to get the results you need. Google Instant is automatically enabled when you search. If you don't want to use Google Instant, click the 'Instant is on' drop down menu to the right of the search bar and select 'Instant is off.' This preference will be saved to your computer, so if you want to use Instant in the future, you'll need to turn it back on.

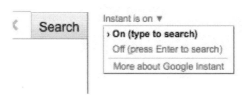

1.5 Language tools

You can set which language you'd prefer your search results to be in. To do so, go to the Google Preferences page (http://www.google.com/preferences) and select your desired language.

1.6 SafeSearch

SafeSearch automatically filters out content Google considers to be explicit, such as pornography and other sexually explicit content. Google uses an algorithm that evaluates a number of criteria, including keywords, links and images. While no filter is 100 percent accurate, SafeSearch has a strong track record for filtering out objectionable content. If you have young children, you may wish to enable this feature. To do so, go to the Google Preferences page (http://www.google.com/preferences). You can choose between three different levels: strong filtering, moderate filtering and no filtering.

Strong filtering filters objectionable search results as well as pages that may link to objectionable results. Moderate filtering only filters explicit images themselves, and is the default setting for SafeSearch. To ensure no one can make changes to these settings, you can choose to lock SafeSearch and apply strict filtering to all searches on your computer using your web browser. SafeSearch works by saving a cookie to your web browser to filter results. If you use multiple web browsers on the same computer (such as Internet Explorer and Firefox), you'll need to make this change in both browsers. If you switch computers, you'll also need to adjust your settings again.

1.7 Time saving Google search short cuts

Google's team of engineers have optimized your search with time saving short cuts:

- **Currency Conversion** – Type the amount and unit followed by the currency you are converting to

  Example: 100USD in EUR

- **Local Businesses** – Type location followed by type of business

  Example: Washington, DC sushi

- **Movies** – To find movie times for your area (if you have already saved your location), type movies. Otherwise include your location

  Example: Movies, NYC

- **Sport Scores** – For the latest scores, simply type in your team or league

  Example: Dallas Cowboys, NFL

- **Time** – To find out the current time in any city worldwide, type 'time' followed by the city

  Example: Time, Bangkok

- **Unit Conversion** – Type the amount and unit followed by the unit you are converting to

  Example: 4 ft in meters

- **Weather** – Type the word 'weather' followed by your US or international city

  Example: Weather, Los Angeles

Chapter 2: Google Calendar

2.1 Getting started.

To get started, sign in to your Google account and go to
https://www.google.com/calendar. Your Google calendar will look like this:

The main window displays your calendar dates. The left side bar displays a monthly view, lists your personal calendars ('My Calendars') and underneath your shared calendars ('Other calendars').

There are several ways to navigate Google Calendar. To get started, select one of the buttons in to upper right corner of the Calendar page: Day, Week, Month, 4 Days and Agenda.

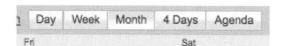

You can choose the dates you want to view by using the arrow buttons in the upper left corner of the page. Or, pick a date range in the mini calendar on the left side of the page. You can also view additional calendars by clicking on that specific calendar name from the calendar list. If a calendar is highlighted with a colored bar, it is being viewed. Click the calendar again to toggle it off and remove from view.

2.2 Customizing your calendar

To add an event to your calendar, simply click once on the day. An event box will pop up where you can name and create your event.

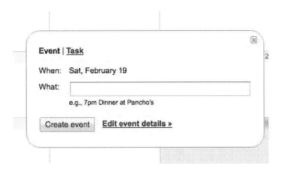

To edit event details, click the 'edit event details' link or if you are in the main calendar view, double click on your event. Doing so will open the following menu:

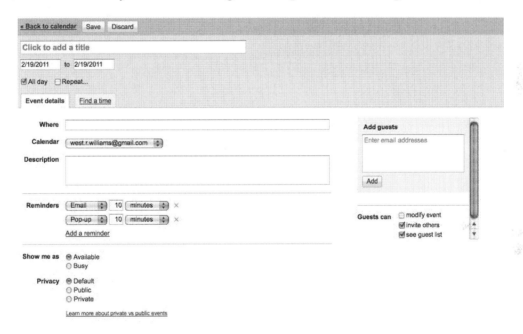

Enter your event information, a brief description and an event reminder. You can add guests to the event by entering their email address and clicking 'Add.' You can customize the privacy settings to determine whether guests can invite others, see the guest list or modify the event.

2.3 Sharing your calendar

1- In the calendar list on the left side of the page, click the down arrow button next to a calendar, then chose 'Share this calendar'

2- You can also click the Settings link at the bottom of the calendar list, then select a calendar and chose the 'Share this calendar'

3- Enter the email address of the person that you want to share your calendar with.

4- From the drop-down menu, select a level of permission, then click 'Add.'

5- Once you click 'Add,' the person that you selected to share the calendar with will receive an email invitation to view your calendar.

You can currently share your calendar with up to 75 users per 24-hour period. If you need to share with more users, you will need to wait 24 hours before doing so.

You can also share calendars with a group of people via Google Groups. The calendar sharing settings will automatically adjust to any changes in the group's membership over time. To learn more about Google Groups, see Chapter 5.

2.4 Adding a calendar

To add a friend's calendar, enter their email address in the 'Add a friend's calendar' field at the bottom of the calendar list on the left and hit enter. If your friend has opted to share his or her calendar publicly, their calendar will appear under 'Other Calendars' in your calendar list. If not, a message requesting access to your friend's calendar will appear. Add a note if you want, and click 'Send Request.'

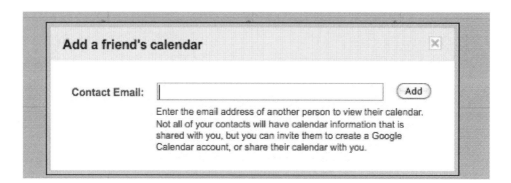

You can also add interesting public calendars. Click Add -> 'Browse Interesting Calendars.' This will open a menu where you can browse and preview interesting calendars such as international holidays and sporting events.

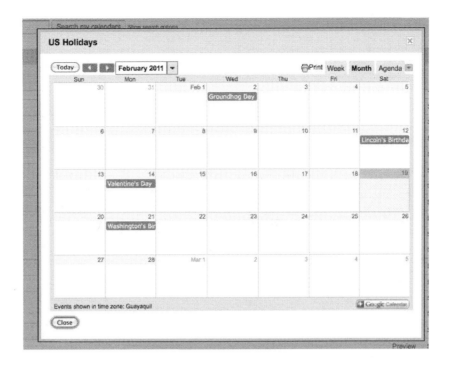

Chapter 3: Gmail

Gmail is different from other email services you may have used in the past. With Gmail, you have virtually unlimited storage capacity and can access your email from anywhere in the world. Instead of deleting emails, you can archive them with Gmail (think of it as storing your email in a virtual filing cabinet that's always organized and never fills up). Even better, instead of organizing your mail by folders, you'll organize your mail with labels. This way you can have more than one label for each email. Gmail's powerful spam filter keeps unwanted emails out of your inbox. You can chat with contacts directly in Gmail via chat and video chat, and even make phone calls. You can access Gmail through your web browser, or receive emails in Outlook and other email clients, on your smart phone or as a text message. This section covers the basics of getting started with Gmail, how to customize the interface and organize your email and advanced features.

3.1 Getting started.

To get started, login to Gmail at www.gmail.com. If you don't have an account you'll be prompted to create one.

When you first log in to Gmail, you'll see the following screen:

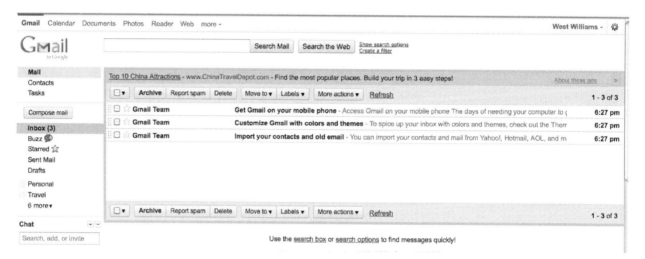

Your inbox: This is where you can see the messages that you have. To open a message, simply click on the line. New messages will appear in bold in your inbox. To see all unread messages, type **is:unread** in the search bar.

Buttons: This row of buttons helps you manage your messages; this row is at the top and bottom of your inbox.

- **Select:** Use this button to quickly select a certain set of messages on the page. You can select all messages, only those that are unread, or only those that are starred.

- **Archive:** Click to Archive (see 3.3)

- **Spam**: When you report an email as spam, Gmail responds by blocking similar messages. The more spam the Gmail community marks, the smarter Gmail becomes at detecting and avoiding spam. If you see a spam message, click Report Spam. Sometimes, a message may end up in the

Spam folder by accident. If this happens, click 'Not Spam' to move it back to your inbox. Messages that are in Spam for more than 30 days are automatically deleted.

- **Delete:** Check the box to the left of a message and click this button to delete it and move it to the Trash. Messages that are in Spam for more than 30 days are automatically deleted

- **Important/Not Important:** Flags for priority inbox (see 3.3)

- **Move to/ Labels:** Label messages (see 3.3)

- More Actions: The 'More actions' drop down menu is where you can star a message, mark it as unread, read, etc. To perform one of these actions, select the message(s), click the 'More action' button and click the task.

Left Sidebar: Here you can switch between your Mail, Contacts and open your Task list. When you are in Mail mode, the menu below will display links to your Inbox, Priority Inbox, Starred messages, Chats, Drafts etc. You will also see links to your Labels. In Contact mode you can add a new Contact and see links to display your different contact groups and import contacts.

Mail Sidebar: **Contact Sidebar:**

3.2 Customizing your inbox: choose your own theme

Your Gmail inbox defaults to a specific theme. To change the theme, go to Mail Settings -> Themes. You can choose from preset colors and photographs or select your own colors combination.

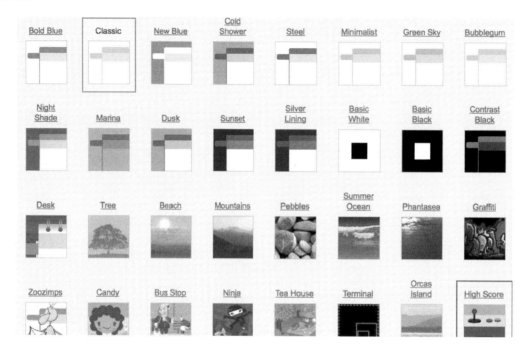

Standard v. HTML view. By default, when you access Gmail through a web browser, your inbox will display with the standard view. If you have a very slow connection or your browser does not support all the Gmail features, you can switch to HTML view. This will disable certain features (such as chat, spellcheck and filters) and the interface will be simplified, but you will still be able to read and send emails.

3.3 Organizing your inbox: conversation view, archiving, labeling, filters and priority inbox.

Conversation view: Gmail organizes your emails by conversations or threads. Conversation view means that emails of the same topic will be grouped together, rather than kept separately in your inbox. When you reply to an email or receive a reply back, these messages will be kept together on the same line in your inbox with a number next to them (such as 2 or 5) to indicate how many messages are in the conversation.

When you open one message in a conversation, all of the related messages will be stacked on top of each other, from the newest on top to the oldest on the bottom. Gmail calls this 'conversation view.' To view a message, simply click the conversation and hit 'Show All.' This is a handy and quick way to follow responses and comments made to one topic (especially when multiple people are on the email chain), rather than searching through your inbox for each message.

Conversation view is automatically enabled in your Gmail account. If you'd prefer each message to display individually in your inbox, click the Gear icon and select 'Gmail Settings.' Under the 'General tab' click 'Conversation view off.'

Archiving. When you don't want to delete a message but also don't want to see it in your inbox (and it's just not worth labeling), archive it. Archiving a message moves it to 'All Mail.' You won't have to see it in your inbox, but if you need it, you can still search for it, and it will appear under any labels you have applied to it.

Labeling. Gmail doesn't use folders; it uses labels. Labels are similar to folders, except that you can add more than one label to a conversation. For example, if you receive an email from a coworker that contains information about a project assignment and details about her new favorite restaurant, you could label it both as 'work' and 'weekend plans.' You can add as many labels as you'd like to a conversation. Even better, adding multiple labels to an email doesn't mean you are making multiple copies of the same message (with folders, if you wanted to file an email in two spots, you'd need to have two copies). Think of it as sticking multiple labels on a single piece of paper: less clutter and more organization.

To add a label, click the '**Labels**' drop-down menu and select the check box next to the label(s), or click '**Create new**' to add one. To assign a label to a conversation, highlight the conversation and click the desired labels from the drop down menu. You can access all the messages in a label by clicking the label on the left side of your Gmail page.

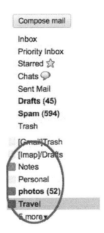

Filters. Your inbox just got smart. Using Gmail's filters, you can manage the flow of incoming messages, automatically labeling, starring, deleting, archiving or keeping a message out of the spam folder. A filter is a combination of criteria such as keywords, sender, recipient, attachments and more that tell Gmail how to sort your incoming email. You can also use a filter to automatically forward specific messages.

1. To create a filter, click the 'Create a filter' button (yes, it's that tiny blue text next to the 'Search the Web' button at the top of the page).

2. Enter the criteria for your filter. For example, you may wish to enter work email addresses to ensure all emails from your boss get labeled 'Work' so you don't miss them.

3. Perform a 'test search' to determine which emails in your inbox currently match the filter's criteria. This is a great way to determine whether your filter is effective or needs to be tweaked.

4. When you create a filter, only new incoming messages will be affected. If you'd like the filter to affect messages already in your inbox, after you perform a test search you will need to select the '**Also apply filter to x conversations below' option.**

5. **To edit or delete a filter, click the Gear icon and select 'Gmail Settings.'**

6. **Select 'Filters' and click the desired filter to make changes/delete. When you are finished, click 'Update filter.'**

A few notes about using filters to forward email:

- **If you use a filter to forward email messages, only new messages will be affected.**

- **Before any messages are forwarded to a new address, you will need to verify that you own the account.**

- You can create an unlimited number of filters, but only 20 can be used to forward messages.

You can also use Boolean operators in the keyword fields to make your filters more precise and accurate. For more on Boolean operators and a list of useful operators, see the section on searching Gmail.

Priority inbox. Priority inbox works like a filter, in the sense that it moves your most important messages to the top of your inbox and adds a tiny yellow tag to these messages. If you activate priority view, when you login to Gmail you'll see a separate 'priority box' above the rest of your inbox that holds your important, unread messages. Priority inbox automatically flags email from senders you are frequently in contact with (via email or chat) or that contains keywords that are also in other emails your frequently open. You can also train priority inbox to be smarter. If it misses an email, simply flag it yourself. If it flags an unimportant email, remove the flag. Over time, priority inbox learns what is and is not important based on your feedback.

3.4 Contacts: create, import, export and organize

Your contacts are shared across your Google account, so if you add or delete a contact in Gmail, the contact will also be added/deleted in other applications.

Create. Every time you send an email or hit 'Reply', 'Reply to all,' or 'Forward,' the addresses on your email will be automatically added to your Contacts list. If an email lands in your spam folder and you mark it as 'not spam,' Gmail will also add that address to your contact list as well. To manually enter a contact, select 'Contacts' from the left side of your screen and click 'New Contact' from contact manager. Any information you add will be automatically saved. To add information to a contact, such as a phone number, address, birthday or website, simply click on the contact in contact manager.

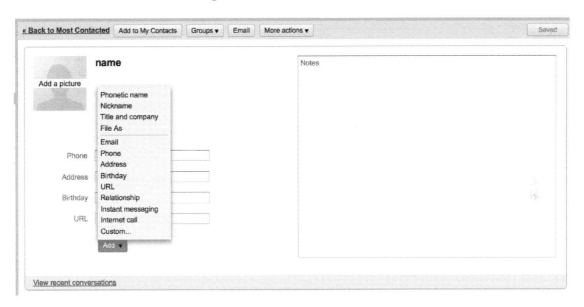

Import. If you already have other email accounts, you can take your contacts (and even your old email) with you to Gmail. Gmail supports import from a number of accounts including AOL, Hotmail, Yahoo and other webmail and POP3 accounts.

1. Click the Gear icon and select 'Gmail Settings.'

2. From the Accounts and Import tab, click 'Import mail and contacts.'

3. Under 'Step 1', you will be prompted to sign into your other email account and enter your password.

4. Under 'Step 2,' you can select your import option. You can choose to (1) import contacts, (2) import mail, (3) import new mail for 30 days, and (4) add a label to all imported mail. Click 'Start Import' when you are ready.

5. Your contacts and email (if selected) will now be imported. It can take up to 48 hours for email to show up in your account, so don't panic if you do not immediately see your messages.

Note: if you want to import your messages but also leave the original copies on the old mail server, be sure to check this option. Gmail typically uses 'TrueSwitch' to import contacts and messages, which will never delete messages from the server of your old account. However, if Gmail is unable to import with 'TrueSwitch,' it will notify you that it is using 'Mail Fetcher.' In this case, you'll need to check the box **'Leave a copy of retrieved messages on the server.'**

Import from Outlook. You've spent years organizing your business contacts in Outlook. Now you can easily take them with you to Gmail.

1. Open Outlook. Click File -> Import and Export.

2. Select 'Export to File' and click 'Next'

3. Click 'Comma Separated Value' (CSV) and click 'Next'

4. Choose a location on your computer to temporarily save the file, enter a name, click 'OK' and then click 'Next'

5. To customize your export, click 'Map Custom Fields.' You can select how much (or how little) of the information in your contact fields are saved.

6. Click 'Finish' and confirm your file is saved to your computer

7. Log in to Gmail from your web browser. In the left column click 'Contacts'

8. Click 'Import' and browse to find and select your saved file

9. Click 'Open' and then click 'Import Contacts'

Export. It's easy to take your Gmail contacts with you.

1. From the Contacts page click the 'More Actions' drop-down menu and select 'Export.'

2. You can choose whether to export all contacts or only one group.

3. Select the format for export. If you are migrating contacts from one Google account to another, use the 'Google CSV' format. If you are moving contacts to Outlook, Mail or another web-based email client, use the 'Outlook CSV' format. To transfer contacts to your Apple address book, use the vCard format.

4. Click 'Export' -> 'Save to disk' -> select a location on your computer to save the file -> click 'OK'

Organize. Contact Manager includes several default groups to help your organize your contacts. These groups are:

• My Contacts – Addresses that are important to you, such as close friends and family. You may not use these the most, but they clearly matter most.

• Most Contacted – The 20 addresses you contact the most, automatically updated by Gmail.

- Friends, Family, Coworkers – Additional default groups that are empty until contacts are added

- Other Contacts – Contacts you have not organized

To create a new contact group, click Contacts -> Groups -> Create New. Enter the name of the group and click 'OK.' To add contacts to your new group, check the contacts you wish to add from your contacts list. Select your new group from the 'Groups' drop down menu. If you have multiple addresses saved for a contact, you can choose which address should belong to the contact group by opening the contact and clicking the small arrow next to the group you'd like to modify.

3.5 Searching Gmail

Some people love to carefully organize their contacts, label their emails and create filters to easily find important messages. Other folks prefer to keep everything in one giant inbox (and with virtually unlimited storage space, that's generally not a problem). But no matter how carefully you do (or don't) organize your messages, at some point you'll need to search them for information. The search box is located at the very top of your inbox screen.

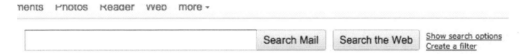

You can use the Gmail search function just as you would use Google. Type in a word or phrase, and Gmail will pull up every instance that phrase appeared, with the search term highlighted in yellow. You can also use advanced search operators to make your search criteria more specific. To use advanced operators in your searches, click 'Show search options' to the right of the search field, and enter your search terms and advanced operators in the appropriate fields. A list of useful Boolean operators is below.

Operator	Definition	Example
from:	Specify sender	from:west
to:	Specify receiver	to:erin
subject:	Searches for words in subject line	subject:dinner

OR	Search for terms matching 'A term' OR 'B term'	from:westORwilliams
- (hyphen)	Exclude term from the search	subject:dinner –plan
"" (quotes)	Search for an exact phrase	"dinner plans"
label:	Search by label	subject:dinner label:restaurant
has:attachment	Only messages with attachments	subject:dinner has:attachment
filename	Search by name or type of file	filename:ProjectReport.pdf filename:pdf
in:inbox in:trash in:spam	Search for messages in a specific folder	in:inbox from:west
is:starred is:unread is:read	Search for messages that are starred, unread or read	is:read from:west
after: before:	Search for messages based on a date (yyyy/mm/dd format)	after:2011/01/15

3.6 Using Gmail in Outlook

Gmail can be accessed via Outlook Express, Outlook 2003 and Outlook 2007. To set up Gmail for Outlook, be sure you have enabled IMAP in your Gmail settings. You can do this from

Settings -> Forwarding and POP/IMAP -> IMAP access. Just make sure the 'Enable IMAP' button is selected. Don't forget to click 'save changes' when you're done.

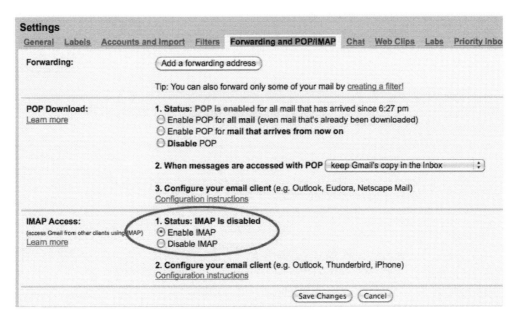

NOTE: These instructions are tailored for Outlook 2007; Outlook 2003 and Outlook Express are similar. Gmail also works with Apple Mail and Thunderbird.

1. Open Outlook and select 'Add new email account'

2. Enter your name, email address (including '@gmail.com'), and password.

3. At the bottom of the setup box, select 'Manually configure server settings or additional server types' and click 'Next'

4. Select 'Internet Email'

5. In the 'Internet E-mail settings' window, under 'Server Information' select the following:

   a. Account Type: IMAP

   b. Incoming mail server: imap.gmail.com

   c. Outgoing mail server: smtp.gmail.com

6. Enter your User Information and Logon Information and select 'Next' to save and finalize account setup.

You will still need to add additional information:

1. From the Tools menu, select Options -> Mail Setup

2. Click 'E-mail accounts'

3. Select the Gmail account and click 'Change'

4. Click 'More Settings' and then select the 'Advanced' tab and add the following:

   a. Incoming server must be 993, and must use SSL encryption.

   b. Outgoing server must be 587, and must use TLS encryption.

5. Click the 'Outgoing Server' tab and select the following:

   a. 'My outgoing server (SMTP) requires authentication'

   b. 'Use same settings as my incoming mail server'

6. Click 'OK' -> 'Next' -> 'Finish' -> 'Close' -> 'OK'

For faster downloads, turn off your email client's spam filter! Gmail's spam filters also work in your IMAP email client, so you do **not need to** enable your client's junk mail filters. In fact, Gmail recommends that you disable any additional anti-spam or junk mail filters within your email client. If you leave on additional filters, your email client's filter will attempt to download and classify all of your existing messages, which will significantly slow down your email times. There's no need for double spam filters, and in all likelihood Gmail's are a lot better than your existing client's filters.

3.7 Gmail on your phone

Gmail can be configured for your smartphone, including iPhone, Android, Blackberry, and other popular phones. To use Gmail on any smartphone, make sure you have enabled IMAP in your Gmail settings. (See 3.6 for information)

Gmail for iPhone, iPod Touch and iPad:

1. Open the Settings App on your device

2. Tap 'Mail, Contacts, Calendar'

3. Tap 'Add Account'

4. Select Gmail

5. Enter your account information, including the '@gmail.com' part of your address

6. Tap 'Next' and 'Save' – you're all set up!

Gmail for Android:

1. Press **<Home>**, then open the **Email** application.

2. From the 'Your Accounts' page, select 'Next' to begin setup

3. Enter your Gmail address and password and select 'Next'

4. Give your account a nickname and chose the name to display on your out going messages

5. Tap 'Done' – you're all set up!

Gmail for Blackberry:
NOTE: Gmail is not officially supported for Blackberry at this time. You can follow the steps below or download the Gmail mobile app for fast access. Learn more at blackberry.com/gmail

1. Go to the home screen

2. Select the email setup icon (depending on which Blackberry you have, this may be called Setup, Setup Wizard, Email Setup, BlackBerry Set-up, E-mail settings, or Personal Email Set-up)

3. Follow the setup instructions on your device

3.8 Sending Gmail to your phone via SMS

Using email forwarding and filters, you can send email to your phone as an SMS message. This is a great filter to activate if you don't have a smartphone, but still want to know when you receive an email from an important family member, friend or client. As with all text messages, you'll be charged the regular fee from your service provider, so unless you have an unlimited SMS plan or don't receive a lot of email, be sure to set up the address filter.

First, set up the forward to your phone. Under Mail Settings -> Forwarding and POP/IMAP select 'add a forward' and enter your 10 digit cell phone number followed by your service provider's text message address. Popular addresses are below:

AT&T: 10digitphonenumber@mobile.att.net

Verizon: 10digitphonenumber@vtext.com

T-Mobile: 10digitphonenumber@tmomail.net

Sprint: 10digitphonenumber@messaging.sprintpcs.com

Next, set up a filter. When you set up the filter, list under 'From' the addresses that are the important ones you'd like to see. Click 'Next.' Click the 'Forward it' option under 'Create a filter.' As with email-to-email forwarding, you will need to verify the forwarding address for your email to be forwarded.

Chapter 4: Google Reader

4.1 What is Google Reader?

Google Reader is a web-based aggregator that reads Atom and RSS feeds from websites. It then displays the latest content from your favorite sites all in one place. It's like your own personalized inbox for your favorite web sites. And because Google Reader constantly checks your favorite news sites and blogs for content, whether a site updates daily or monthly, you won't miss a thing – and you won't waste valuable time checking up for updates yourself. With Google Reader, you don't have to give any personal information, it's free, and it's easy to unsubscribe from a feed at any time.

Even better, you can share postings with friends on Google Reader simply by sending them the relevant link. Post items of interest to your 'shared items' folder and your friends can see them too. If you have a blog or website, you can add a customizable clip that displays your latest shared items in your site's sidebar. You can also "follow" friends, so their latest postings appear in your inbox along with your Atom and RSS feeds.

4.2 Getting started with Google Reader

Websites publish lists of updates, called "feeds," that indicate when new content has been posted. When you subscribe to a feed, Google Reader starts monitoring that feed for updates.

Finding feeds. Start with the websites you visit every day. Do you have a favorite news site? Does your cousin write a blog you love to read? Whatever the site, simply type the address into the 'Add Subscriptions' link and Google Reader will find the feed. Some sites have multiple feeds, so make sure you choose the main feed and not, for example, the comment feed (unless of course that's the feed you want.) You can also look for words on the site that indicate a feed, such as subscribe, syndicate, rss, xlm, and atom or look for the feed logo in your browser's address bar. You can also search the Google Reader directory for new and interesting feeds based on your interests.

Adding feeds. Once you know the address of the feed you want to subscribe to, just click the '**Add Subscriptions**' link and paste the address in the text field that appears.

If you are switching from another feed reader, you can import your existing subscriptions into Google Reader. To do so, first export your subscriptions in OPML format. In Google Reader, click 'Settings' in the top right corner and select 'Import/Export', select the OPML file and click 'Import.' Google Reader will automatically add your subscriptions and begin checking for updates.

Removing feeds. If you no longer want a feed, you can unsubscribe. To do so, click on 'Settings' in your Subscription list. Check the box next to any feeds from which you no longer wish to subscribe. Click the 'Unsubscribe' button.

Reading your feeds. New content from your feeds will appear in Google Reader the same way that new emails appear in your email account. You can click through the different stories and select which ones to read, just as you would your email.

1- Add subscriptions- Click here to enter the URL address for a website

2- Your 'inbox' – This lists all your latest feed updates, items you've shared, notes and trash (Yep, just like a real inbox!)

3- People – Gmail contacts who you follow that are posting to Google Reader. A 'New!' will appear next to a contact who has just posted something.

4- Subscriptions – A list of all your current feed subscriptions. Click 'Manage subscriptions' to remove feeds. To view items only from a specific feed, select that feed here.

5- Your 'inbox' where you can view feeds, just like you'd read email messages. If you like a feed, you can share it; see the next section for more information. You can also 'star' it (just like in Gmail). Starred items will appear in your starred list (accessible through the left menu).

4.3 Sharing and following

Sharing your feeds.

If you like something you read in a feed, you can share it with your friends or post it publicly. Before you share something, you can add your own notes and comments. To share something, click the '**Share**' button underneath the item. You can choose only to share the item or to share it with notes.

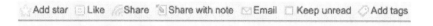

To manage your privacy settings, click 'Sharing settings' from the left side bar and select 'Who can see my shared items' from the drop down menu. You can choose between public or protected; protected items are visible to your friends. You can specify which friends you wish to share with by selecting a list from your Google contacts.

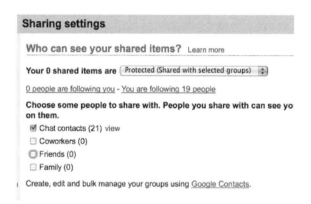

Following friends. To find out who you are following (if you follow someone you can see their shared items in your feed), click the 'Sharing Settings' link under the 'People you follow' box. At the very top, it will say 'You are following X people' and 'X people are following you' where 'X' is the number of people. Click on one of these links to see which friends you are following and which friends are following you. Keep in mind that even if a friend follows you, they won't be able to see your shared posts unless they are on one of your sharing lists (or you have your sharing settings on public).

Chapter 5: Google Groups

5.1 What is a Google Group and how is it different from other list serve groups?

A Google Group is a user-owned and created group that connects people and helps them share information over the web in a secure, user-controlled environment. Google Groups allows you to manage and archive your email list as well as create customizable web pages for sharing information with the group. Unlike other free list services, Google Groups offers large (and free!) storage limits as well as the ability to customize your own web pages just for group members – you aren't limited to just email communication. Google Groups also never displays annoying banner or pop-up ads (only relevant text ads).

Google Groups can be used for a variety of purposes. Whether you want to plan your next family reunion, collaborate on a group project, or learn more about a hobby and find others who share your interests, Google Groups provides the tools for you to connect and exchange information in a constructive dialogue.

5.2 Getting started: joining a group, posting messages and replying

To get started with Google Groups, sign in to your Gmail account and visit http://groups.google.com/. You'll see a home page that lists your current groups memberships (if any), your profile (with stats like how many postings you've made), suggestions for other group memberships and the ability to search all Google Groups.

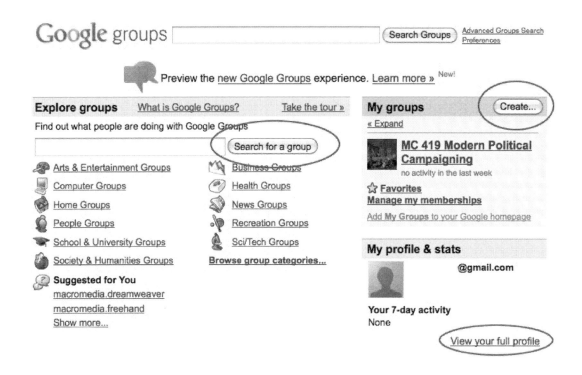

Joining a group. You can join a group (also known as 'subscribing') via email or through Google Groups. To subscribe to a group through Google Groups online, log in to your Google Account and visit the group of your choice. If you aren't sure what group you want to join, you can search for the group. For example, searching Google Groups for 'photography' will bring up all groups that are about photography. You can further sort through the results based on region, topic, messages per month, number of members and language. Click the "Join this group" link on the right-hand side of the page under "About this group."

Search options for photography groups:

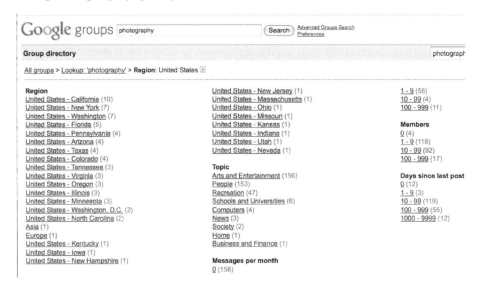

This group is restricted; click the 'Apply to join group' link at the top for membership:

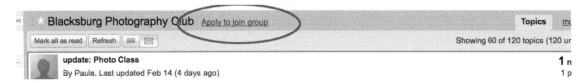

You can also subscribe to a group via email. To do so, send an email to [Groupname]+subscribe@googlegroups.com. Some groups are membership-restricted. If you wish to join a membership-restricted group, you will need to wait for the group administrator to approve your request.

Alternatively, you may receive an email invitation from a group administrator to join a Google Group. To accept, simply click the link in the email and follow the instructions.

Viewing messages. As a Google Group member, you can choose to have group messages sent to your email account. You can also view messages online at the Google Group site:

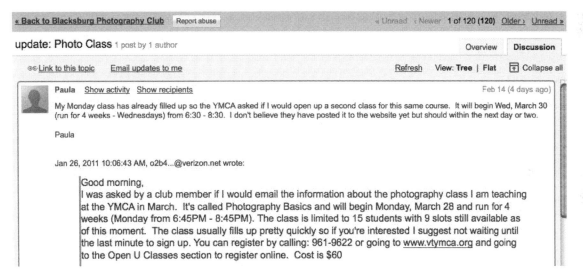

Posting messages. Once you are group member, you can post messages to the group. (In some cases you may be able to post messages even if you are not a member). To submit a post via the Google Groups page, visit the group's homepage and click the '+ new post' button in the 'Discussions' bar on the right side of the page. To reply to an existing topic, click 'Reply' near the bottom of the posting. To submit a post via email, send an email to your group's email address. The email subject line will be the subject of the post and body of the email will be the content of the post. If posting is restricted, your post will be reviewed by a moderator before it is publicly available to the group.

Replying to messages. You can reply to messages over email or through the Google Group page. To reply over email simply hit the 'reply' button in your email program. Type your reply into the body of the email. Be sure to keep the subject line the same so your reply is included in the correct thread. To reply to a post through the Google Group page, simply hit the reply link at the bottom of the post. To reply directly to the author simply click the 'Reply to author' link at the bottom of the post.

5.3 Creating your own Google Group

If you already have a group email list, it's easy to migrate this list to Google Groups. To get started, go to http://groups.google.com/, sign in to your account and select the 'Create Group' option from the 'My Groups' tab:

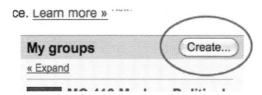

You will now need to set up your group with a name, an email address, a brief group description and choose an access level for content. Next, you can add members by importing an existing email list or manually inviting people.

Adding members. To add members, follow these steps:

1. Click Invite members from your group's homepage.

2. Select the 'Add members directly' tab.

3. Add the email addresses of the members you'd like to add to your group, separating each email address with a comma.

4. Write a welcome message for your new group members.

5. Select a default subscription setting for your group members under Email subscription options. They'll be able to change these settings later if they have a Google Account.

6. Click 'Add members.'

Your members will be listed as 'non-verified' until they accept their group invitation and verify their email accounts. If members are 'non-verified' they cannot receive email.

Owner v. Manager. The person who creates the Google Group (in this case, you), is known as the 'owner.' This is the person who created the group, invited the first members, and chose the privacy/posting settings. The owner can also elevate members to 'manager' status. A manager can approve posts, invite new members, create managers, and change the group's management settings. Only the owner, however, can create a co-owner, transfer ownership to another user or delete the group.

Chapter 6: Google Sites

6.1 What is Google Sites?

Google sites is a web-based application that allows you to collaborate with other people to quickly and easily create a site by sharing file attachments and information from Google applications (everything from YouTube and Picasa to Google Calendar and Google Docs.) Whether your site is for a high school English class to share homework assignments and announcements, a student club or a team project, a way to stay connected with family or a secure company Intranet, you can create your own Google site with a few clicks of the mouse – no html code required. Privacy settings allow you to designate other collaborators who can post material and control who can see your Google site (just a few people, a whole organization or the entire world).

6.2 Getting started with Google Sites.

Creating a Google site is just like creating and editing a document. You can choose from a variety of premade themes and tailor them to meet your needs. Sign in with your Google account at https://sites.google.com and click the giant blue 'Get Started' button. You'll begin by choosing a template (you can also opt to create a page from scratch), selecting a name for your site and a url address (all sites will have the url prefix (https://sites.google.com/site/).

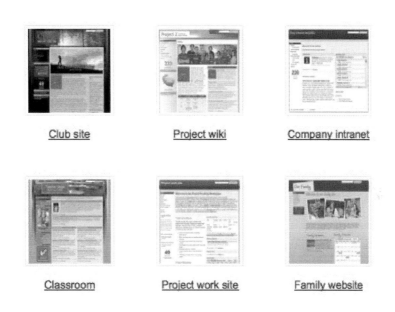

Club site   Project wiki   Company intranet

Classroom   Project work site   Family website

Set your privacy by choosing who can view your site. Later, you'll be able to grant access to individual people.

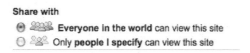

Click 'Create Site' and you're ready to go!

6.3 Editing and managing your site

When you first create a site you'll see your theme or template display with sample text and images you can edit as needed. In the example below, we created a sample project page.

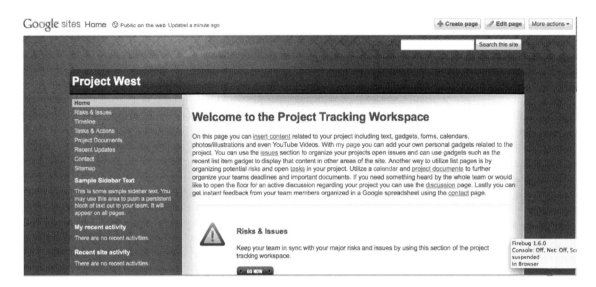

To make changes to the layout, such as the sidebar, click the 'edit sidebar' link. This will open a new window where you can edit and revise the text, links and images in your sidebar.

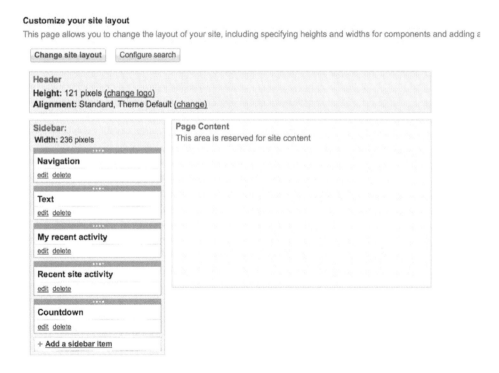

The top right corner has three key menu buttons. Click 'Create Page' to add a new page to your site. Click 'Edit Page' to edit the current page you are on. Click 'More Actions' to view your revision history, save the current page as template, share the site and more.

6.4 Using Google Sites for your business.

Google Sites is a secure and powerful way to build a company intranet, company training site, project management site and more.

- **Company Intranet:** Use your site to post company news, link to retirement and health care benefits information, integrate with Google calendars and create a separate section for each department.
- **Project management:** Get your project organized in a central place and easily manage deliverables, review and share documents, and track deadlines with Google calendar integration.

- **Training:** Run your company training from one central place. Add training material and test pages, a calendar with a training schedule, link to useful resources and get feedback from employees.

- **Small business site:** Give your small business a professional, online presence. Add testimonials, product samples, a blog, a Google map showing your location, and more.

- Document library and sharing: This basic site allows you to store and share documents securely across your company. Ideal for companies with telecommuting, you can now keep all your important files in one place and access them from anywhere – no expensive sever sharing software required.

- Resume and portfolio: Working as a freelancer? Searching for your next job? Give yourself a professional, online presence. Post your resume, create and update a portfolio and include links for potential employers to contact you.

6.5 Using Google sites for your personal life.

Google Sites is not all work and no play – they are a great way to stay connected with family, friends and others who share your interests.

- Club: Are you a member of your local hiking club? Do you get together every Thursday night with friends for a book club? Keep track of your club's activities here. Post photos from your hikes, discuss your latest book, and add a directory with member's contact information.

- Family: Create a personal site for your family, whether it's just for you and the kids or for your entire extended family. Post photos and videos, share schedules and plan your next family reunion.

- Home projects: Finally going to remodel the kitchen? Looking to landscape your yard? Keep your home projects organized on one central place. Collect and save ideas for your projects, add a timeline, integrate with Google calendars and post photos and videos of your renovation.

- Neighborhood: Ever tried organizing a neighborhood event but ran into too many scheduling conflicts? Get your neighborhood online and organized in one place. Plan events with Google calendar, add announcements, link to local community resources, add a directory with neighbor contact information and post photos and videos from neighborhood events.

- Team: Coaching your daughter's soccer team this year? Keep all the team information in one place. Use Google calendar to update practice schedules, Google map to show practice and playing field locations, post photos and video from the games, and keep track of who's bringing the post-game snacks.

- Travel journal: Keep family and friends connected if you're traveling abroad. Include a blog for posting your adventure stories, a calendar to track when you've been where and the ability to insert videos, photos and link to your Facebook and Twitter accounts.

- Wedding: Track and share all the details of your big day in one place. Allow guests to RSVP online, link to your registries, post engagement photos, share your 'how we met' story and post your bridal party.

Chapter 7: Blogger

7.1 What is Blogger?

Blogger is Google's free tool for creating blogs. It's different from Google Sites because Blogger is designed to be primarily a single page, or an online journal.

7.2 Getting started with Blogger

You can set up a Blogger account with three easy steps.

1. Sign in with your Google account.

2. Name your blog.

3. Choose a template.

You can host multiple blogs with the same account name, so you only need to sign up once. This way you can have a separate professional blog that's different from say, your blog about traveling in South America, which is also different from your family reunion blog.

Once you are all set up and log in for the first time, your home screen will look like this:

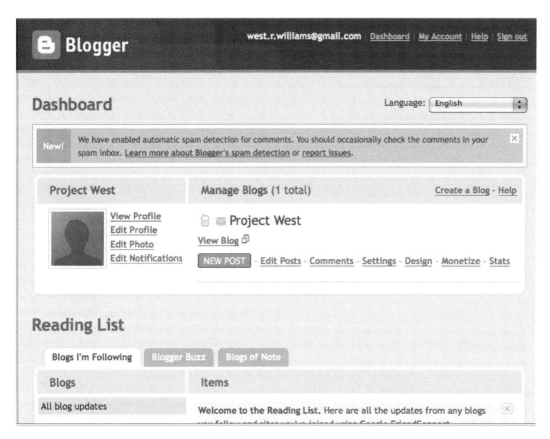

Dashboard: Manage your blog by creating and editing blog posts, tracking your stats and comments, and editing your blog design. You can also edit your blogger profile, add a photo and edit your notifications.

Reading list: This tracks blog updates for other blogs you are following, blogger buzz and blogs of note.

To create a blog post, click the Posting tab and select New Post. You can compose your post using Blogger's WYSIWYG (what you see is what you get) editor, or if you have experience with html, you can also edit/compose your post in html code. Simply click the 'html' tab to switch. Be sure to preview your post before publishing!

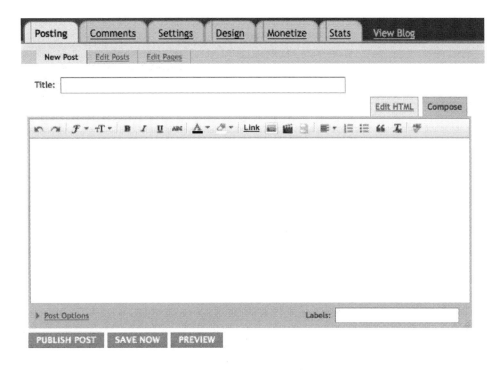

You can also configure Blogger with an email address, so you can email your posts to your blog. This is a great way to post quick updates from your cell phone or another mobile device. Or you can use the Blogger mobile app from your smartphone.

7.2 Tips for customizing your blog

To edit the design of your blog posts, click 'Design' from the main dashboard or the 'Design' tab. You can customize the placement of different page elements, edit your header and add a gadget. To personalize your blog, you can upload a custom header you design yourself. You can use this header in place of blogger's standard 'title and description,' use the header as a background image for the title and description, or have the description appear after your new header image.

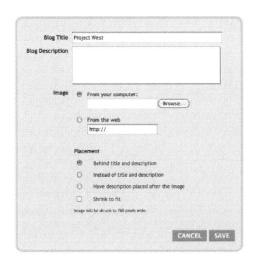

A gadget is a snippet of html code that adds functionality to your blog. Examples include a search box, slide show, video bar, picture poll, and a link list to other blogs. Gadgets are an easy way to add embedded videos and add images to your site – and you never have to worry about coding anything!

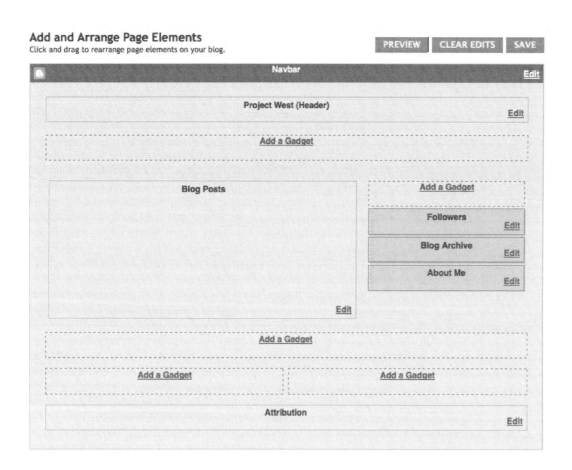

Adding videos and images. You can upload photos and video from your computer, add photos and video to a gadget (as discussed above) or post photos to your blog directly from Picasa web albums.

7.3 Managing your privacy.

Click on the 'Settings' tab to manage your account settings, including privacy. By default, your account is added to Blogger's listings and search engines can find your blog. If you want to keep your blog private (and only share a link with individuals who have verified credentials) click Permissions. Here you can enter who can read your blog (up to 100 specified people) and who can post to your blog. By default everyone can read your blog (unless you change this setting) and only you can post to your blog.

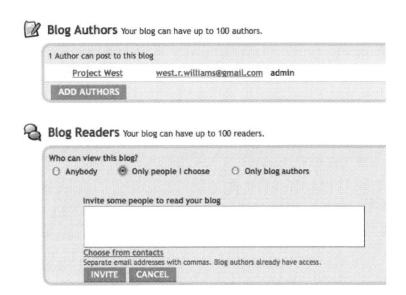

7.4 Monetize your blog

Is your blog popular? Is it really, really popular – and not just with family and friends but with people in your community, state…even folks you've never met that live across the country? If you get a lot of blog traffic you can turn these hits into dollars by monetizing your blog.

Google's AdSense will place ads automatically on your blog page. The amount you earn depends on your subject matter and the popularity of your blog. You can choose how you want ads to display on your blog, or you can chose to display no ads at all. The amount you earn depends in part on how much web traffic you receive (the more traffic you receive, the more likely that companies will want to post ads and that people will click on the ads). You'll get paid when your earnings reach a certain threshold. In the US, you are paid when your earnings reach $100.

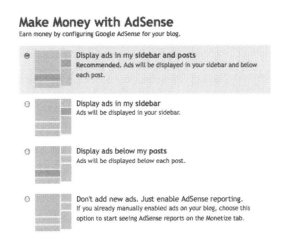

Chapter 8: Google Shopping

8.1 What is Google Shopping?

Google shopping puts the power of Google's search engine to work for your wallet, helping you compare prices and search products. Formerly known as Google Products and Froogle, Google Shopping was officially launched in 2007 and has been helping folks find bargains ever since.

Google Shopping is different from most price comparison services because it does not charge any fee for lists and will not accept payments to alter search results (and ensure certain products display first). It also does not make a commission on sales. Any company can submit products for inclusions via Google Shopping APIs.

If you have used Google to search the web (or searched just for photos or videos), using Google Shopping is no different. Instead of searching 'Everything' you'll only be searching relevant shopping listings.

8.2 Getting started with Google Shopping

To get started, go to Google.com and click on 'shopping' from the top left menu.

Now Google will display 'shopping' results for any item you search for – helping you compare brand, store, price and even free shipping. The example below shows a search for "iPhone case." This broad search has returned over 1.6 million results, which Google has ranked by relevancy.

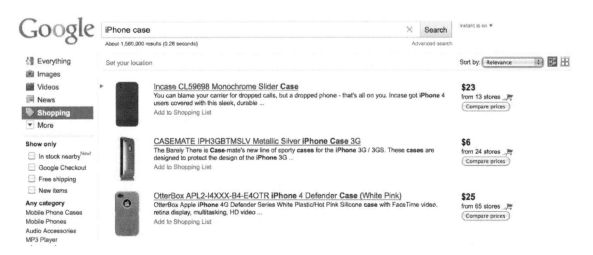

The main search result column shows the product, and the right column shows the price and where it is available. You can also click 'compare prices.' You can sort the results by relevance, price: low to high, and price: high to low.

In the left column, you can further narrow your search results by selecting products that are in stock nearby (you will need to specify your location first for this feature to work), offer Google check out, have free shipping, or a new item. You can also narrow the results by selecting a category, in this case "Mobile phone cases" or "Basketball fan accessories" depending on what you're looking for (very useful if you want an iPhone case with your favorite NBA team on it!) You can select price ranges (such as up to $15, $15-$30) or manually enter your own price range. You can also choose between brands and stores.

When you are ready to buy, simply click on the search result and pick your online check out destination.

Chapter 9: Google News

9.1 What is Google News?

Google News is a news aggregator that uses Google's page-ranking search algorithm to rank news reports, just as the Google search engine ranks search results.

9.2 Getting started with Google News

To use Google News, go to Google.com, type in your search term and click on the 'News' tab in the top menu bar. Your search results will only include 'News' results rather than 'everything' results. The example below displays results for the term 'iPhone.'

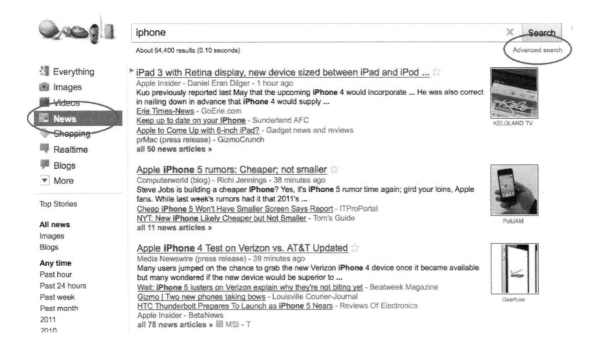

9.3 Advanced Google News Search

In the example above, we simply searched for the term 'iPhone.' But what if we want results only from a specific date range or a specific news source (such as the New York Times)? Click the 'Advanced' button under the search box to further customize your search options. You can search for the specific term containing all the words, the exact words, at least one of the words or add a 'without words.' For example, if you want stories on the iPhone but ones that are not about apps, you could enter 'iPhone' into the 'with all the words' field and enter 'apps' into the 'without the words' field. You can further customize your date range, the time the article was added to Google News, your news source, source location, your location (so you only get articles about your local area), author, and number of keyword occurrences.

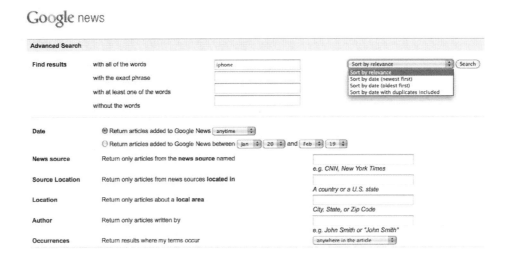

9.4 Setting up Google News Alerts

When you search a specific term, Google includes a link to set up a news alert on that term at the bottom of your first page of search results.

Stay up to date on these results:
- Create an email alert for **iphone**

An email alert is then sent whenever news matching your topics is published online. You can customize your Google News Alerts by selecting the source (news, blogs, video, realtime, discussions), the delivery method (email or feed – feed will go to your Google Reader page) and the volume (best results as determined by Google or all results). To further edit your Google News Alerts (and remove old or unwanted alerts) go to http://www.google.com/alerts and sign in to access your account.

9.5 Using News Archive Search

Google News also includes a feature called 'News Archive Search', which allows you to search historical archives going back more than 200 years. The depth of access varies based on the news source, and you may have to pay to see some of the full stories (this is determined by the news source). For example, you can access the New York Times all the way back to its founding in 1851. To use this feature, click Archives or enter a custom date range in the left menu bar.

Archives
Custom range...
From: 1/1/2000
To: 1/1/2005
ex: 5/23/2004
Search

Chapter 10: Google Docs

Introduction

How Google Docs can help you keep your business sane

We are about to undergo an important shift in the way companies and individuals use applications to get work done. In the early days of computing, there was only one option. We had to use software installed on the computers at the office. For a long time, this approach worked just fine. But as the Internet grew to be more rich, it also began to support increasingly complex web-based applications. These days, there is a cheaper and more efficient way to handle office and personal documents. It's called Google Docs.

Google Docs is a web-based office software suite that gives you the same tools as Microsoft Office and Apple's iWork, all for zero cost. You can create word documents, spreadsheets, presentations, drawings, and everything else you need to keep your business running smoothly. It's like having an online version of Microsoft Office that works on any machine capable of connecting to the Internet.

Google Docs doesn't just get the job done. It's actually better than Microsoft Office in many respects. With Google Docs, you can easily collaborate and share your work with your co-workers. Gone are the days of sending emails back and forth, asking if so-and-so got such-and-such. It's all online. If Gene didn't get the memo, he doesn't have to ask you for it. He can find it by logging in to his Google Docs account.

That's just one of the handy features that will keep you and your team using Google Docs for a long time. We've found many more that keep us coming back, so many that we wonder why more organizations don't make the switch as soon as possible. Why pay for office-wide software licenses when you can use better software for free?

This guide is for busy professionals who want to learn how to use Google Docs for their business. We've included a section on each office-specific application, so you'll see firsthand how to create documents, presentations, drawings, spreadsheets, and forms. It's all online and 100% free. Stick with us, and you'll never have to buy office software again.

Google Documents

Google Docs contains a fully featured online word processing tool. On a functional level, it's just as good, if not better, than Microsoft Word or Apple's Pages. You can format your documents, print them, and share them with your colleagues when you're all finished. In this section, you'll learn how to put this powerful tool to use so you never have to pay for a word processor again. Let's see how it works.

To use Google Documents, you need to create a Google account.

Chances are you already have a Google account. If you've ever used YouTube or Gmail before, you had to create a Google account to get started. For those of you who don't have a Google account yet, it's very easy to set one up. Just follow these steps.

- **Go to Google.com**. You could've guessed that one, but because there are always a few stragglers, I had to say it.
- **Click on the "sign in" button in the upper right hand corner.** It's kind of small, but it's up there. Here's what it looks like.

- **After you're redirected to the sign in page, click on the "create an account now" link.**

Don't have a Google Account?
Create an account now

- **Fill out the form and follow the instructions.** It's just like every other online thing you've signed up for.

Once you've got your Google account sorted out, you can start working on your first online document. To get there, go back to Google's homepage and click on the "more" button in the top bar. After that, click on "documents" to get started.

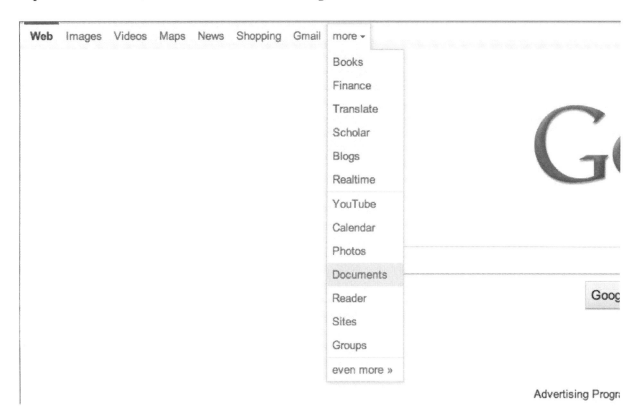

Of course, there are other ways to get there. The most obvious of these is to simply type "google docs" into Google's search bar. It will be one of the first links. In any case, pick whichever works best for you.

Creating your first Google Doc.

If you are logged in, Google will take you right to your Google Docs account. On this screen, you'll see every online document you've created (none so far) as well as a few options you have for organizing all of that content. If you aren't used to storing your files online, the Google Docs user interface will seem a little weird. There are no folders for you to store your documents. You just have a long list of files.

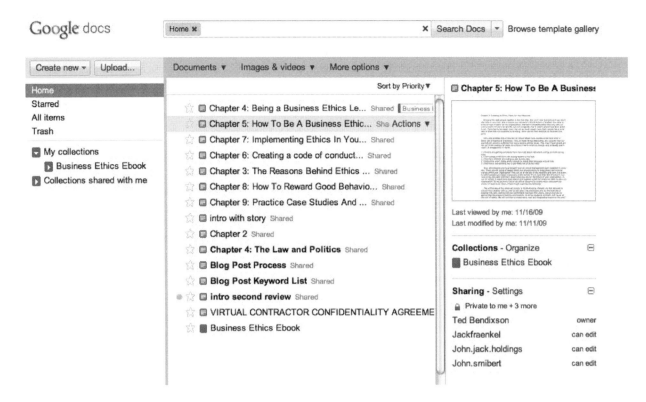

Instead of folders, you have collections. Once you create a document, you can add it to a collection to help you keep things neatly organized by category. But we can get to this part later. For now, we're going to create our first Google Doc.

To do that, click on the "create new" button in the upper left hand corner.

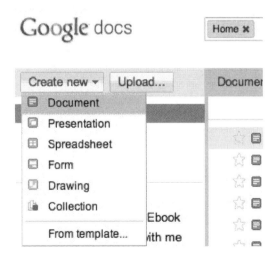

You'll notice that you have quite a few options here. Google Docs isn't just a word processor. It's an entire office software suite, literally an online (and totally free) Microsoft Office. You can do everything in Google Docs that you can do with any of these relatively expensive software packages.

At this point, you'll be taken to Google's Document editor. This is where you do the actual work. Everything is designed to function just like Word or Pages. Most of it should be familiar, so we'll go over some of the more confusing bits.

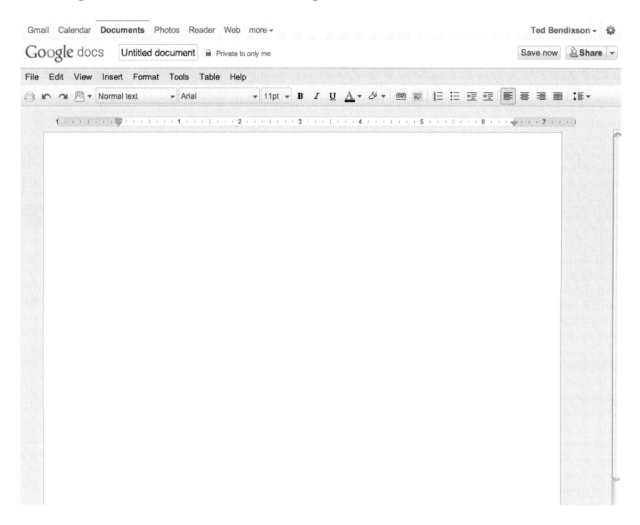

Just for fun, let's assume the American Revolution is taking place in the year 2011 instead of the year 1776. The British have levied heavy fines on Internet usage, and our leaders have had enough. They've decided to collaborate online to create a Declaration Of Independence from the British crown.

Michelle Obama is the leader of the American colonies, and she is going to share the first draft with our nation's first man, Barack Obama. But she won't get anywhere if she doesn't have a title. Let's change that.

How to title your Google Doc.

Have a look in the upper left hand corner of your Google Docs word processor. You'll see a text field that says "Untitled Document." Click on that.

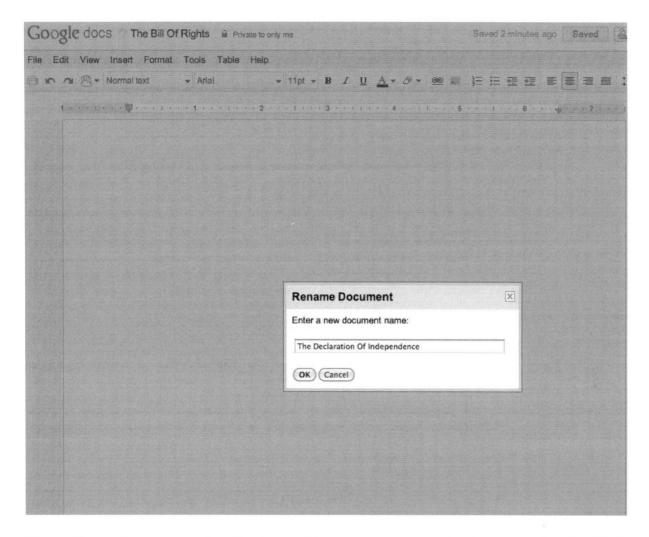

You will now be prompted with a box asking you to rename the document. I picked "The Declaration Of Independence," but you can pick anything you want. Click O.K.

Once you do that, the top bar will change, reflecting the new name you've chosen:

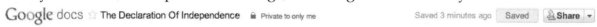

Do you see the text on the right where it says, "saved seconds ago." That's another awesome thing about Google Docs. In a stroke of pure brilliance, the folks at Google have decided to completely automate document saves. As you write, Google saves your project and tells you when it last did this. If you want, you can go ahead and save, but it's practically unnecessary. Google Docs saves after you enter every new word.

To start, we'll create a headline for our document using a sans-serif font. Let's pick something more akin to our writing style. We'll go with Corsiva, using an 18 point font.

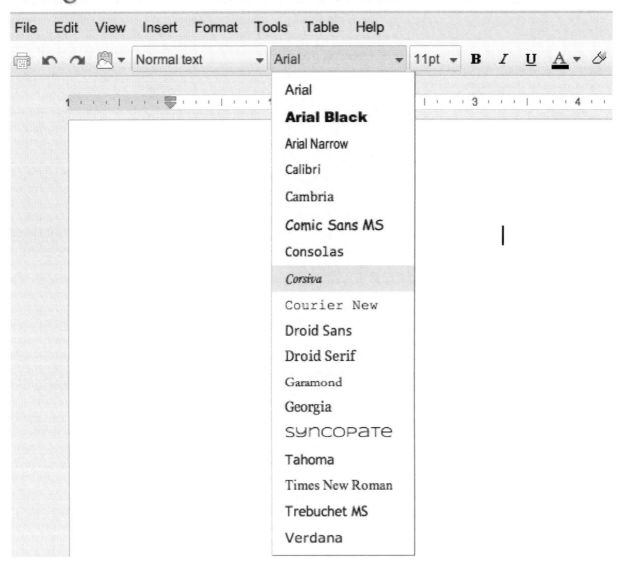

Once again, not too much is different here. You've probably used toolbars like this one countless times before. Familiar icons tend to do what familiar icons do.

Google Docs does have one disadvantage, and that is its fairly limited font family. Thankfully, most of that is changing. Google has added new fonts in the past, and they plan on adding more in the future. What you see is just a current snapshot, and considering that the entire software suite is free, it's not that bad.

But I digress. We'll write the heading and first paragraph of our Declaration Of Independence before we decide to send it off to Barack for review.

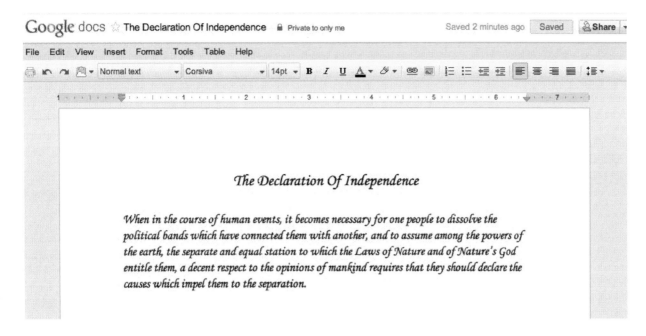

Looks good. But what would happen if we got a power outage (another cunning attack by the Brits), and our computer suddenly shut off? How would we get back to the Declaration Of Independence?

Opening a saved document.

I want you to close every Internet browser window you're currently using. I'm serious here. Do it.

Did you do it? O.K. Now let's go right back to Google.com. Once again, you can either go to "more --> documents" in the upper toolbar, or you can search for Google Docs. Either works.

Because you're still signed into your Google account, Google will take you right back to your list of documents. You should see The Declaration Of Independence at the top of that list.

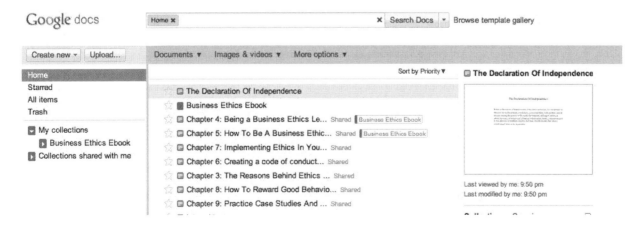

The most recently viewed and edited document gets the top spot. That's why you don't really need to organize your documents with folders. 99% of the time, you'll be working on your most recent project. You'll rarely find yourself going back through your previous work, and when you do, you can just use the "search docs" bar at the top to do it.

When we click on The Declaration Of Independence, it'll open right up in the browser, and we can get back to writing. It's just like opening up a Word or Pages document on your home computer.

At this point, if you have a mobile device like a smartphone or a tablet, go right to your Google Docs account and have a look at your work. Any changes you make while on the go will be saved to the same document. Now you no longer need to keep track of different versions on different devices. It's all online.

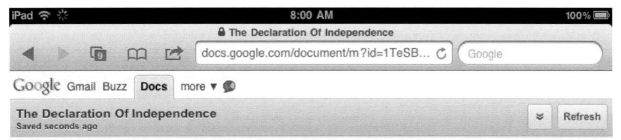

The Declaration Of Independence

When in the course of human events, it becomes necessary for one people to dissolve the political bands which have connected them with another, and to assume among the powers of the earth, the separate and equal station to which the Laws of Nature and of Nature's God entitle them, a decent respect to the opinions of mankind requires that they should declare the causes which impel them to the separation.

We hold these truths to be self-evident, that all men are created equal. And that they are endowed by their creator with certain inalienable rights.

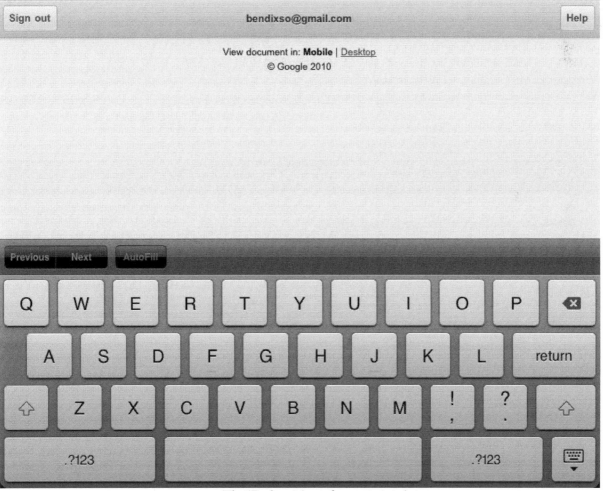

The iPad version of my masterpiece.

The Declaration Of Independence

When in the course of human events, it becomes necessary for one people to dissolve the political bands which have connected them with another, and to assume among the powers of the earth, the separate and equal station to which the Laws of Nature and of Nature's God entitle them, a decent respect to the opinions of mankind requires that they should declare the causes which impel them to the separation.

We hold these truths to be self-evident, that all men are created equal. And that they are endowed by their creator with certain inalienable rights.

The same document now accessed from my laptop.

The mobile Google Docs, as you can see, gets rid of all the frills. When I made my changes, it assumed the same font, but it didn't copy the text size over. That's okay because, when you get back home, you can very easily do all the formatting from the more robust desktop version.

How to share your Google Docs.

Michelle Obama wants a second opinion on her work. She wants to see what the first man thinks. Knowing Barack's fantastic speech writing abilities, she's definitely consulting the right guy. Here's what she does to share her work with her husband.

Do you see the little share button in the upper right hand corner? When you click on that, a share box opens up, and you get a bunch of different options.

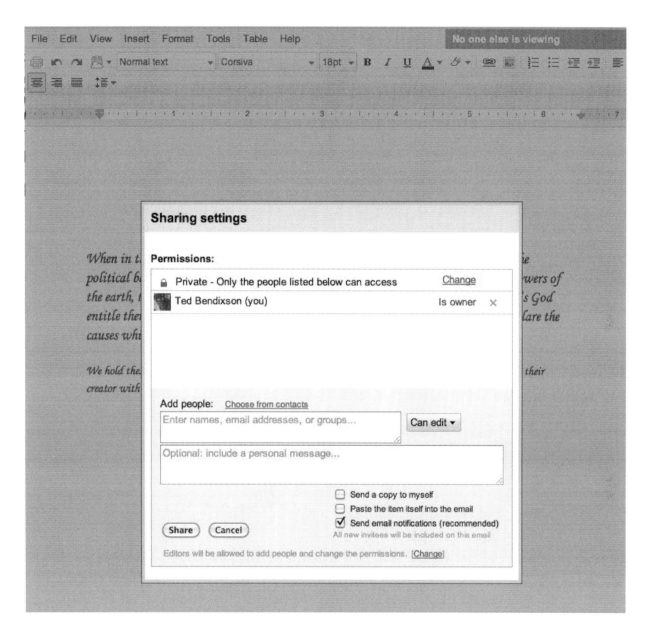

To add someone, you either type in their name or their email address, and Google does the rest. If you use Gmail all the time, you should be able to just type their name, but if you don't, you'll need to do everything via email addresses.

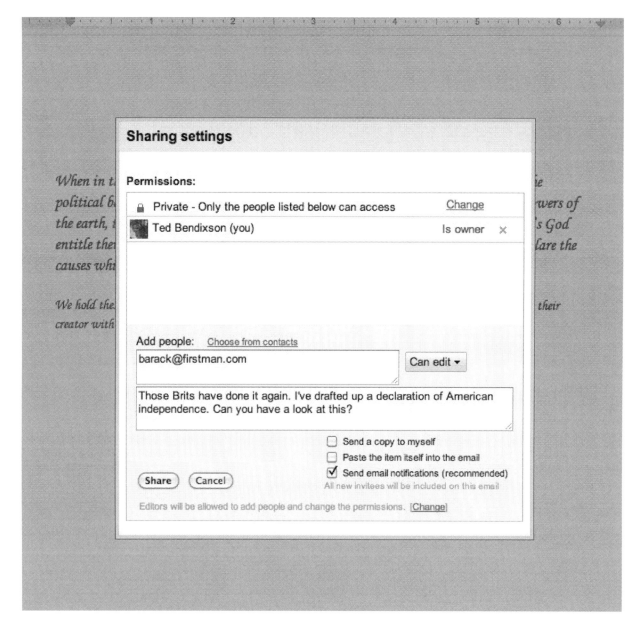

Here's an example of what you can do. When you click "share," an email will be sent to that address, and when the other party receives it, he/she can login to Google Docs to either view or edit the document.

Once you get collaborating with other people online, it gets kind of addictive. Now there's no more sending different versions of the same document across the wires. Any changes you or they make online will be saved automatically, and you can access the document at any time from any device. Cool.

Be aware that not everybody will be amenable to this solution. Some folks are hesitant to create new accounts with Google or any other online company. We'll call them "the old guard," and believe me, they're on the way out. To deal with them, you'll have to do everything the old-fashioned way.

Google Docs allows you to export your work to a Word Document so you don't have to do all of the copying and font processing yourself. Just click on file --> download as --> Word.

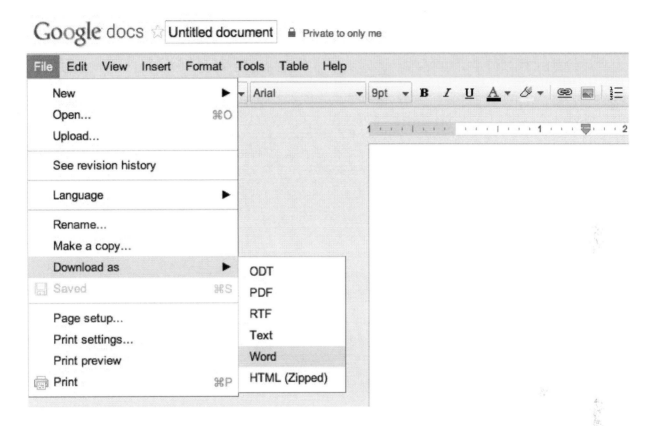

How to edit the work of others and truly collaborate online with Google Docs.

Now we're going to step into the shoes of Barack Obama as he peers over his wife's work. He likes what he sees so far, but he's not so sure about Michelle's tone of voice. Frankly, it seems a little antiquated and not quite befitting a modern leader of the free world. Barack wants to add some comments to Michelle's Declaration Of Independence so she can move her writing in the best direction for our nation.

Here's how he'll do that. To start, he'll select the questionable block of text.

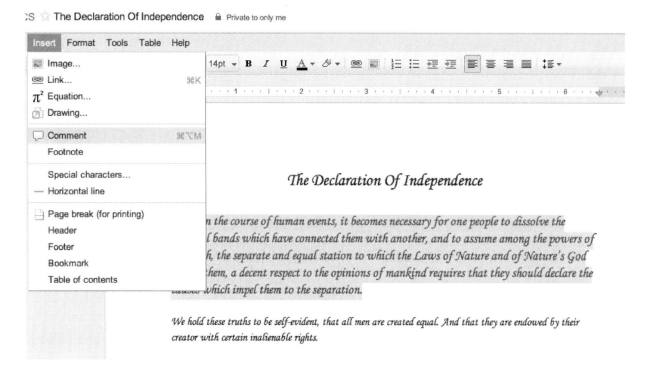

Once he's selected it, he'll go to insert --> comment.

At this point, a comment box will appear in the right margin. If you've ever commented on a Word or Pages document, it's the same thing you're used to. You type in your comment, and it will stay in the margins for others to read. When you print your document, none of the comments will be printed along with it. This is strictly for editing purposes.

The Declaration Of Independence

When in the course of human events, it becomes necessary for one people to dissolve the political bands which have connected them with another, and to assume among the powers of the earth, the separate and equal station to which the Laws of Nature and of Nature's God entitle them, a decent respect to the opinions of mankind requires that they should declare the causes which impel them to the separation.

We hold these truths to be self-evident, that all men are created equal. And that they are endowed by their creator with certain inalienable rights.

Hey honey. I like your direction here, but I think you need to break up this sentence into some more discrete chunks. I'm afraid you might start to lose the attention of your audience toward the end. Love,—Barack

Every member of your team gets his/her own identity when making comments. You can delete your comments by clicking on the trashcan icon to the right. This keeps the workflow nice and clean.

Printing your Google Docs.

After quietly deliberating over her work, Michelle makes some changes to the first paragraph to bring it up to speed with her more modern image. At this point, she's ready to print off a draft to show to the first continental congress. In Google Docs, you never really print to a printer. Your online document, instead, gets saved as a PDF that you can then print from your PDF reader. I know it's somewhat roundabout, but it's the only way to ensure that the formatting is the same.

To export to a PDF, you do what you would normally do while using a standard word processor. Go to File, and then click Print.

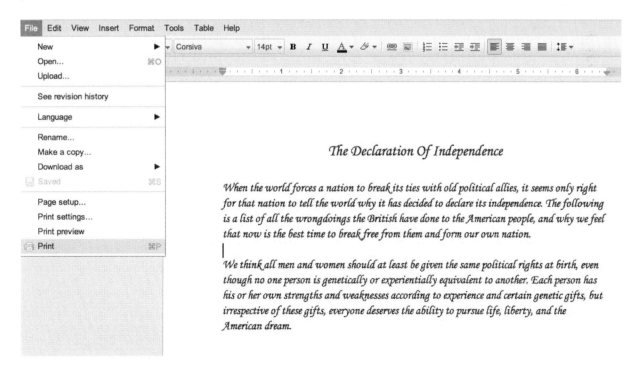

When you do this, you will download your Google Doc, and it will be opened in the PDF reader of your choice. In my case, that's Adobe Acrobat reader.

From there, you have to go to file --> print once more to print to your printer. It's basically the same thing you would do if you were to download any other document from the Internet.

Adding photos in your Google Docs.

Now that you understand the basics of Google document creation, sharing, and printing, it's time to get into some more advanced features. Google Docs works just like any other word processor. You can add in images whenever you want, either by copying and pasting, or by adding them in with the image wizard.

Just find a place where you want to add an image, and click on the little image button in the top toolbar.

This will bring up the image wizard. From here, you can enter a web URL, upload your own photo, choose a photo from one of your Picasa albums, or use Google's image search feature. In this case, we're going to upload our own image.

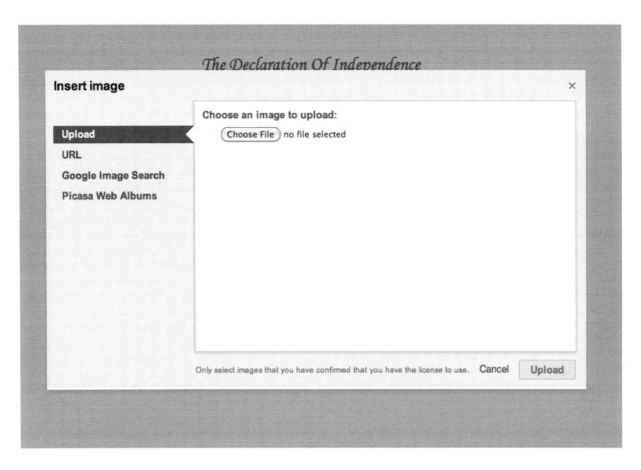

Most smaller images should upload just fine, but be aware that Google has placed some size limitations on your images. You can't upload anything larger than 2000px tall or wide. That includes most pictures taken by a digital camera. Modern digital cameras create images larger than 3000px wide, so you'll need to resize them with some photo editing software before you upload them to your Google Doc.

In my experience, the best practice is to use some screen capturing software to take a small snapshot of the photo you want to include, and then just paste it into your document. That way, you never have to resize anything.

Inserting tables and spreadsheets into your Google Docs.

Tables and spreadsheets can provide a valuable insight into the point you're trying to make with your document. Google Docs allows you to create your own tables or paste them in from a different program like Google spreadsheets. If you're only going to include some light numbers, create the table in your document and fill it out. But if you plan on using built-in math equations to do the number crunching, you'll want to open up a separate document in Google spreadsheets. I'll show you how to do both.

Let's assume for now that we want to provide a basic table stating a few of the British King's infractions committed on the American people. We'll list the infraction as well as a rating signifying the degree to which He has harmed us.

Let's start by going to Table and choosing "insert table." Once you click on this, you'll be prompted to choose the size of the table you want to include. In this case, we'll pick a table size of 2 X 6 to get started.

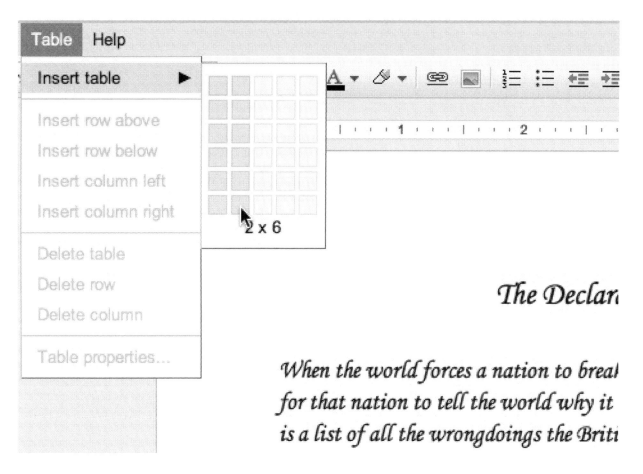

Just like any other word processor, the table is inserted where you last left your blinking cursor. I added a few other things to jazz up our table, but all the basics are there. You just need to add in the data:

The King's Infractions

Infraction	Severity (scale of 1 to 10)
He has refused his Assent to Laws, the most wholesome and necessary for the public good.	3
He has forbidden his Governors to pass Laws of immediate and pressing importance, unless suspended in their operation till his Assent should be obtained; and when so suspended, he has utterly neglected to attend to them.	9
He has refused to pass other Laws for the accommodation of large districts of people, unless those people would relinquish the right of Representation in the Legislature, a right inestimable to them and formidable to tyrants only.	6

As you go along, you can add new rows or columns from the Table menu. Let's add a new column by going to Table --> Insert Column Right.

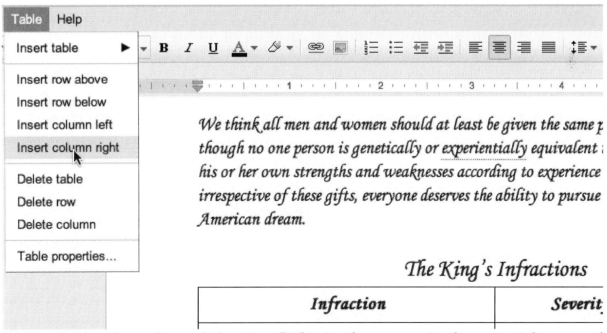

We'll call this column "remedial actions." This is where we write down a quick proposal to remedy the problems the King is creating.

The King's Infractions

Infraction	Severity (scale of 1 to 10)	Remedial Actions
He has refused his Assent to Laws, the most wholesome and necessary for the public good.	3	Create our own laws and pass them by a democratic vote.
He has forbidden his Governors to pass Laws of immediate and pressing importance, unless suspended in their operation till his Assent should be obtained; and when so suspended, he has utterly neglected to attend to them.	9	Institute our own governors with their own power to pass laws.
He has refused to pass other Laws for the accommodation of large districts of people, unless those people would relinquish the right of Representation in the Legislature, a right inestimable to them and formidable to tyrants only.	6	Kill the King and his agents.

Now we can keep on going, adding more rows or columns as the King continues to transgress more boundaries. Our table can be as big as we need it to be.

How to insert spreadsheets from Google Spreadsheets.

Now we're going to take a brief break from Google Docs to check out Google Spreadsheets. The next chapter will go into more detail on Google Spreadsheets, but for the time being, it's handy to know how to create a Google spreadsheet that you can then copy into a Google Doc. This really helps out when you're using Google Docs to prepare financial statements.

Let's go back to the main menu. This time, we'll click on create new --> spreadsheet.

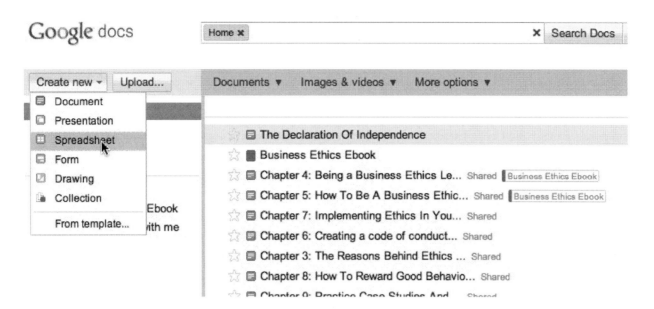

Just like Google Docs, Google Spreadsheets opens up in a completely new window with a blank spreadsheet. We'll call this one "The King's Taxation," and its data will reflect the growing taxes suffered by the American people. It will be a history of Internet taxation rates as a function of time.

You enter data into a Google Spreadsheet in much the same way you enter it into an ordinary spreadsheet. Click on the cell, type in the value, and move onto the next cell. Google Spreadsheets also recognizes when you press tab, so you can quickly move from one cell to the next as you insert new data. Here are some Internet taxation values that Michelle Obama wants to insert into her Declaration Of Independence.

Formula:

	A	B
1	Year	Tax Rate
2	1995	0.01
3	1996	0.05
4	1997	0.1
5	1998	2
6	1999	5
7	2000	5.5
8	2001	5.2
9	2002	5.8
10	2003	7
11	2004	7.1
12	2005	8.1
13	2006	8.3
14	2007	8.43
15	2008	10
16	2009	11.2
17	2010	13
18		
19	Average Tax:	
20	Max:	
21		

Nobody would use a spreadsheet program if it didn't simplify otherwise complex math. We want to get the average of the tax rates over the years so we can present the data to congress. We'll do that by entering a formula for the cell with the pointer hanging over it.

Nearly all spreadsheet programs require you to start a formula by entering the " = " symbol first. So go ahead and do that. You'll notice to something interesting as your start typing " = AV ". Google Spreadsheets automatically suggests a formula for you to type. In this case, it's the AVERAGE( ) formula, just what you'd expect.

Formula: = AV

	A	B	C
1	Year	Tax Rate	
2	1995	0.01	
3	1996	0.05	
4	1997	0.1	
5	1998	2	
6	1999	5	
7	2000	5.5	
8	2001	5.2	
9	2002	5.8	
10	2003	7	
11	2004	7.1	
12	2005	8.1	
13	2006	8.3	
14	2007	8.43	
15	2008	10	
16	2009	11.2	
17	2010	13	
18			
19	Average Tax:	= AV	
20	Max:	AVEDEV(number1, number2, ... number_30)	
21		AVERAGE(number_1, number_2, ... number_30)	
22		AVERAGEA(value_1, value_2, ... value_30)	
23			

Also, just like every other spreadsheet program, Google Docs uses the same syntax to select certain cells. We know that our tax information is contained in the cells between B2 and B17. We tell Google Spreadsheets to calculate the average of those cells by typing in the formula: = AVERAGE(B2:B17), making sure to use a colon to separate the two row values.

Google docs ☆ The King's Taxation ⚐ Priv

File   Edit   View   Insert   Format   Form   Tools   H

🖨 ↩ ↪ 📷 ▾ 🖍 ▾ $ % 123 ▾ | 10pt ▾ | **B** Abc

Formula: = AVERAGE(B2:B17)

	A	B	C
1	Year	Tax Rate	
2	1995	0.01	
3	1996	0.05	
4	1997	0.1	
5	1998	2	
6	1999	5	
7	2000	5.5	
8	2001	5.2	
9	2002	5.8	
10	2003	7	
11	2004	7.1	
12	2005	8.1	
13	2006	8.3	
14	2007	8.43	
15	2008	10	
16	2009	11.2	
17	2010	13	
18			
19	Average Tax:	= AVERAGE(B2:B17)	
20	Max:		
21			

When you press enter, Google Spreadsheets will calculate the average tax rate and place it in the box. You should also have a look at the green selection area. This is a good thing to double-check whenever you're doing any calculations. If the selected area doesn't reflect the values you want to use, you need to change the way you're writing your formulas.

Now that we've calculated an average tax, let's calculate the maximum tax from the same values. I know we don't really need to do this (since we can tell from looking at the spreadsheet), but the practice certainly helps.

Formula: = MAX(B2:B17)

	A	B
1	Year	Tax Rate
2	1995	0.01
3	1996	0.05
4	1997	0.1
5	1998	2
6	1999	5
7	2000	5.5
8	2001	5.2
9	2002	5.8
10	2003	7
11	2004	7.1
12	2005	8.1
13	2006	8.3
14	2007	8.43
15	2008	10
16	2009	11.2
17	2010	13
18		
19	Average Tax:	6.049375
20	Max:	= MAX(B2:B17)
21		

And just like that, our table full of handy taxation data is complete. Now we just need to select it, copy it, and paste it into our Google Doc.

How to copy and paste items between Google Spreadsheets, Docs, and Presentations.
This feature of Google Docs, sadly, isn't the same as what you're used to with a standard word processor. You can't just hit control-c or apple-v to copy and paste a spreadsheet to a word doc. You have to go through Google instead. To do this, you need to use the web clipboard.

You can find the web clipboard in the upper toolbar, next to the heading style box. The icon looks like a little clipboard.

	File	Edit	View	Insert	Format	Form	Tools	Help

Formula: Ye

Copy cell range (20 rows x 2 cols)

Web clipboard help

	Year	Tax Rate	C
1	Year	Tax Rate	
2	1995	0.01	
3	1996	0.05	
4	1997	0.1	
5	1998	2	
6	1999	5	
7	2000	5.5	
8	2001	5.2	
9	2002	5.8	
10	2003	7	
11	2004	7.1	
12	2005	8.1	
13	2006	8.3	
14	2007	8.43	
15	2008	10	
16	2009	11.2	
17	2010	13	
18			
19	Average Tax:	6.049375	
20	Max:	13	
21			

As you can see from this image, I have selected my spreadsheet table and clicked on the clipboard. If I then copy the 20 by 20 cell range, I'll be able to paste it into The Declaration Of Independence document using the same web clipboard. Let's give it a try.

Make sure you give this process a little time, especially if you're going to copy a lot of data. Google Docs will tell you that it is copying the data to the clipboard, using a brief message at the top.

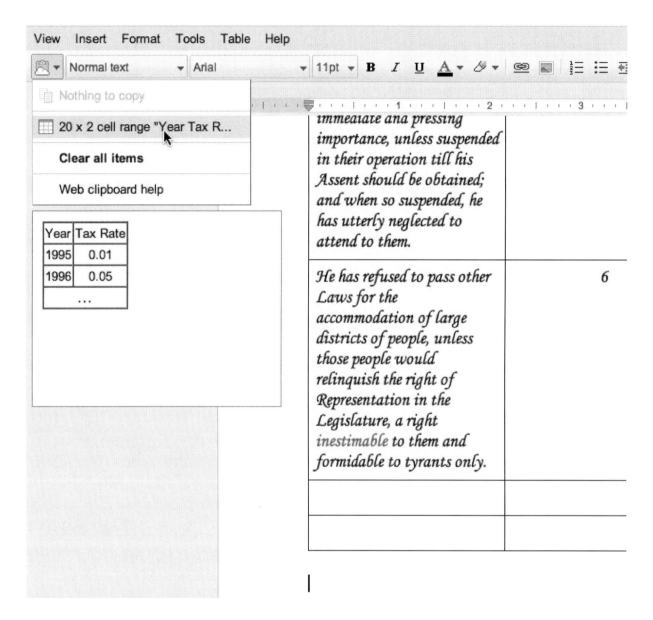

When we paste our data into the document, Google Docs gives us a quick preview so we know we're doing the right thing. Unlike other clipboards, the Google Docs clipboard allows you to copy multiple items at the same time so you can easily put documents together at will.

But wait, what's this? When you paste your table into your Google Doc, it's too skinny. Is there anything you can do to make it look normal?

Year	Tax Rate
1995	0.01
1996	0.05
1997	0.1
1998	2

Don't worry. There is. You just have to click and drag the edges of the table to your preferred width. That includes the middle line as well.

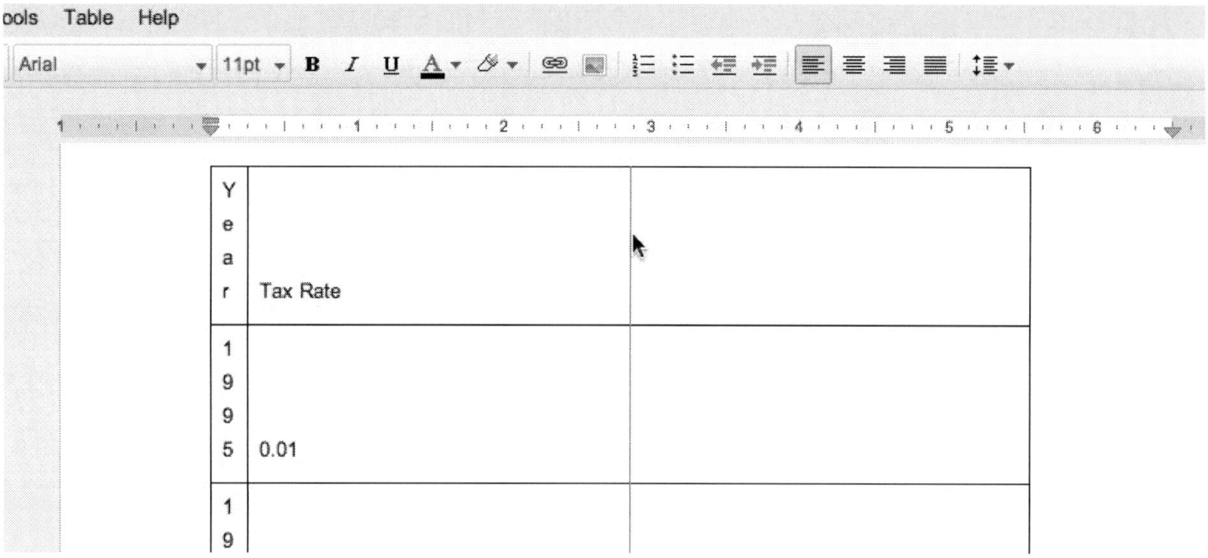

Year	Tax Rate	
1995	0.01	
19		

When you're all done moving things around, your table will look just as it did in your original spreadsheet.

Year	Tax Rate
1995	0.01
1996	0.05
1997	0.1
1998	2
1999	5
2000	5.5
2001	5.2
2002	5.8
2003	7
2004	7.1
2005	8.1
2006	8.3

That's handy. Throughout the course of this guide, you'll learn that there are many other things you can include in your document. Google Docs allows you to paste drawings, equations, forms, and pieces of presentations, all with the same clipboard. It's just as easy, if not easier, to do the same things you did with other word processors in Google Docs instead.

Out of ideas? Consider using a template.

Just like Pages and Microsoft Word, Google Docs features a bunch of different templates that allow you take care of any office or writing project. To access them, just go to the file menu and pick new --> from template.

From there, a new browser window will launch with all of your template options. Google doesn't make the templates. They allow other Google Docs users to upload their favorites. You're looking at templates that real users use all the time.

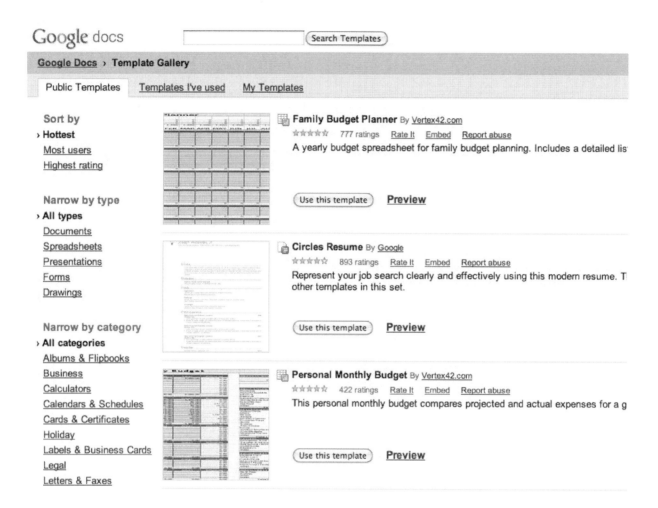

Right now, our templates are sorted by the most popular first. It seems that everyone loves the Circles Resume, so let's give it a try. You can preview a template before you use it, or you can just start using it right away. We'll click on "use this template."

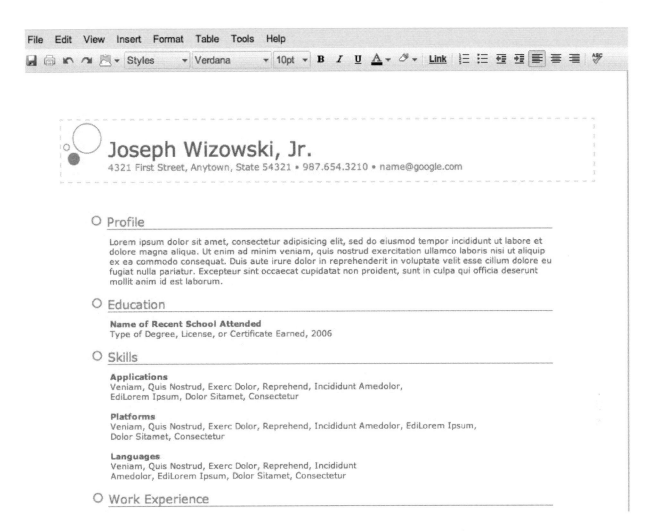

And there you go. You don't have to do any formatting. You can just enter the information yourself. Also, because this is an online Google Doc, you don't need to send it to anyone. You can share it with prospective employers who can then login to view it and comment on it. If your employer wants to know about a specific skill set, he/she can ask all the right questions by using comments.

Have a look at all the other templates, and I'm certain you'll find something to help you cut out a bunch of unnecessary labor. Not bad for a program that costs absolutely nothing.

Onward to the next section.

By now, you should be getting the feeling that your old word processor just isn't necessary, and frankly, isn't nearly as powerful as Google Docs. You've done everything you can do in any ordinary word processor, and now your work is completely decentralized. You can edit the same document on the go as long as you have a stable connection to the Internet. That's pretty awesome.

Now that you know the basics of document creation, sharing, copying, and printing, it's time to learn a little more about Google Spreadsheets. In the next section, we'll get into some more advanced spreadsheet functions. We'll show you how to keep track of important financial goals and create charts that you can embed in your other Google Docs.

Numbers are everywhere in life, and now you never have to lose track of them. When you move all of your spreadsheets online, it makes life a lot easier. There will be no more "did you get the memo?" Now it's online and there for everyone to see.

Google Spreadsheet

In the last section, we gave you a preview of what you can do with Google Spreadsheets. We showed you an example table with a few basic formulas you can use to calculate averages, maximums, minimums, and more. The following section will continue right where we left off, so if you haven't read the chapter on Google Docs yet, go ahead and do that right now. There's a lot of basic information that will help you understand what we're about to discuss here.

To bring you back up to speed, Google Spreadsheets is a fully fledged online spreadsheet program that's meant to do exactly the same thing that Microsoft's Excel and Apple's Numbers do. Because it's online, you can share your spreadsheets with your colleagues, allowing them to either view or edit your work. Just like Google Docs, Google Spreadsheets helps you avoid the hassle that can go along with sending files back and forth. Now you no longer have to keep track of versions because you'll only have one file to work with.

We left off with a made up example table of the British King's Internet taxation rates as a function of time. We calculated an average tax rate, and a maximum tax rate that we pasted into our new Declaration Of Independence. Just to refresh your memory, here is a screenshot of that table. If you were following along in the last chapter, you should have a saved Google Spreadsheet with this data.

Formula:	Year	
	A	**B**
1	Year	Tax Rate
2	1995	0.01
3	1996	0.05
4	1997	0.1
5	1998	2
6	1999	5
7	2000	5.5
8	2001	5.2
9	2002	5.8
10	2003	7
11	2004	7.1
12	2005	8.1
13	2006	8.3
14	2007	8.43
15	2008	10
16	2009	11.2
17	2010	13
18		
19	Average Tax:	6.049375
20	Max:	13
21		

Now that we've got all the data, why not do something with it? The American people undoubtedly appreciate great rhetoric and statistics, but fancy colorful charts can really bring a point home. Let's take our taxation without representation data and make it come alive with a chart.

How to create a chart based on your data.

Charts are something you'll be using all the time in your business, especially in presentations. To make a chart from a table you've already created, you need to start by selecting the data you want to use. In this case, we're going to use the data in columns A and B, and we'll exclude the numbers we've calculated at the bottom.

File	Edit	View	Insert	Format	Form	T

🖨 ◌ ◌ 🖼▾ 🖌 | $ % 123 ▾ | 10pt ▾

Formula: 13

	A	B
1	Year	Tax Rate
2	1995	0.01
3	1996	0.05
4	1997	0.1
5	1998	2
6	1999	5
7	2000	5.5
8	2001	5.2
9	2002	5.8
10	2003	7
11	2004	7.1
12	2005	8.1
13	2006	8.3
14	2007	8.43
15	2008	10
16	2009	11.2
17	2010	13
18		

With all the data selected, we'll then click on the chart button to bring up a list of suggested charts based on our data. The chart button is located in the upper toolbar, and it looks like a miniature bar graph.

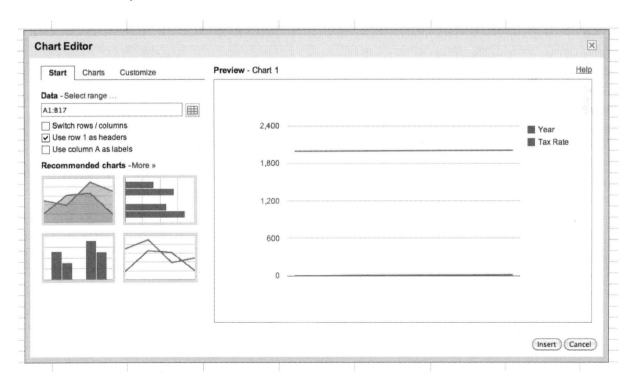

	A	B	C	D	E
1	Year	Tax Rate			
2	1995	0.01			
3	1996	0.05			
4	1997	0.1			
5	1998	2			
6	1999	5			
7	2000	5.5			
8	2001	5.2			
9	2002	5.8			
10	2003	7			
11	2004	7.1			
12	2005	8.1			
13	2006	8.3			
14	2007	8.43			
15	2008	10			
16	2009	11.2			
17	2010	13			

The chart editor has a bunch of different options to help you get the right chart with the data you're giving it. You'll notice that the suggestions we're given seem a little strange. Why are there two lines, for example? Shouldn't the graph simply show an increasing tax rate as a function of each year?

It certainly should, but Google Spreadsheets thinks we want to do a side-by-side comparison of the year and the tax rate, as if the two were somehow correlated. But we don't want to show a correlation between the year and the tax rate, we want to use the year as a label axis to show an increase in taxes as a function of time. To do that, we'll check the "Use column A as labels" button.

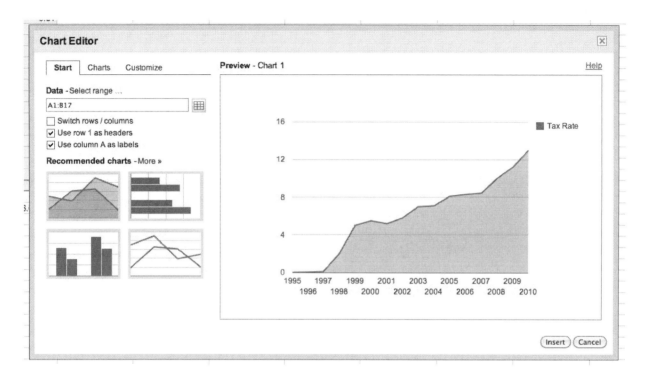

There. That's more like it. Now we can see the steady increase in tax rates as a function of time. Have a second look at the recommended charts. If you don't like what you see right now, you can try a bunch of different visual representations of the same data.

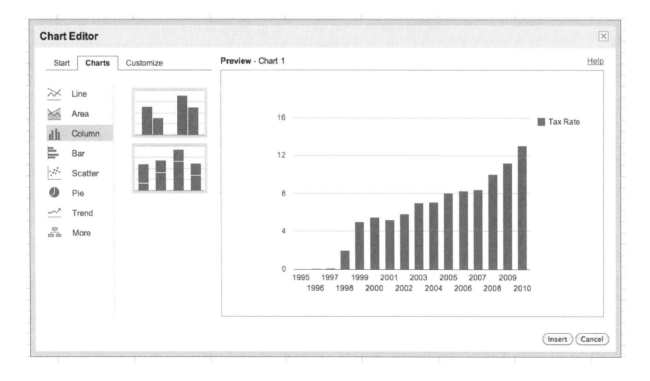

That's pretty cool. I think we've found the chart we want to use, so let's click on insert. When you do this, Google Spreadsheets generates the chart and places it inside of a floating window that you can drag anywhere you want around your spreadsheet.

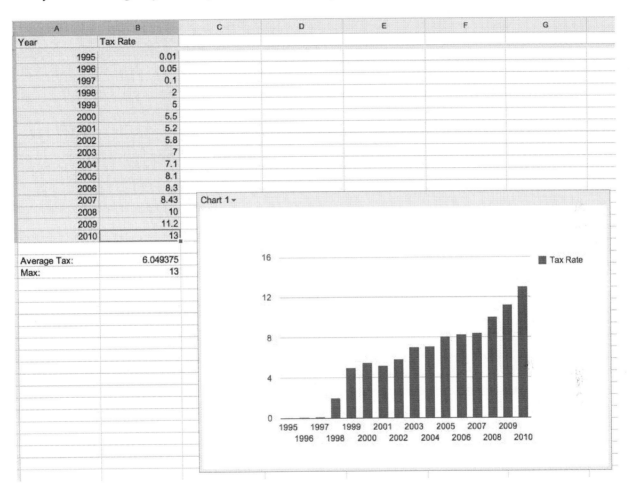

You have a few other options too. If you click on the upper left hand corner of the chart, you can go back to the chart editor, save your chart as a graphic, publish your chart to a website, or move your chart to its own spreadsheet. I decided I wanted give the chart a name, so I went back and added one under the "customize" tab.

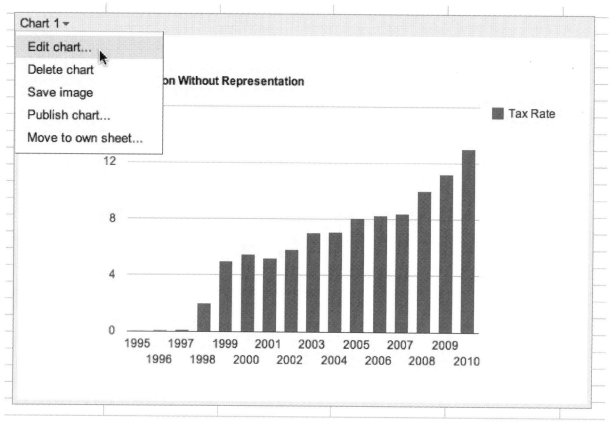

If you decide to save your chart as a graphic, your browser will automatically download it and place it into your downloads folder. This is handy for your clients who aren't onboard with Google Docs quite yet. Also, just like Google Docs, you can always download your spreadsheet as an Excel file by going to File --> Download As --> Excel.

If you choose the "publish to website" option, you'll be presented with a bunch of code that you can paste into any HTML document. Those of you with Wordpress sites will find this quite handy. Just open up the page, paste the HTML, and you're done.

You can also simplify the HTML to an image file instead an interactive chart. Just switch the format to image.

How to paste a chart into a Google Doc.

Those of you who want to paste your chart into a Google Doc will find no luck with Google's web clipboard. You'll have to download the chart to a folder you can remember, and then you'll have to upload and insert it into your document. Here's a quick series of screenshots showing you part of this process.

1.)

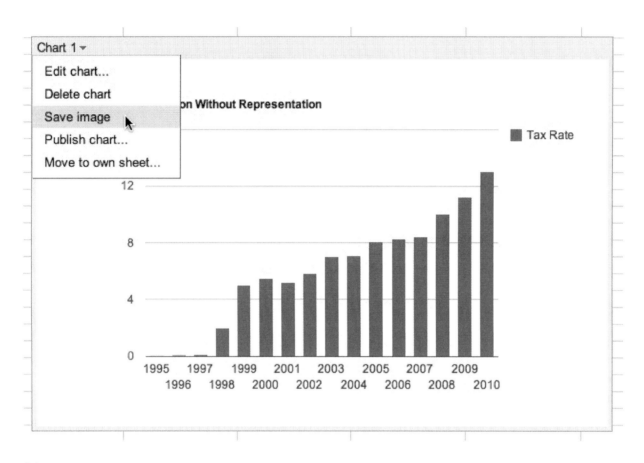

2.)

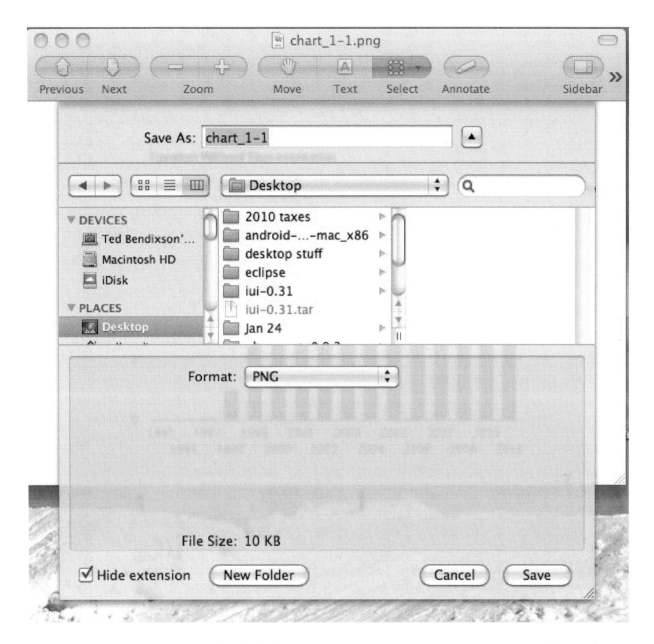

Mac OSX opened the downloaded chart in preview, so I went to Save As and saved it as PNG on the desktop.

3.)

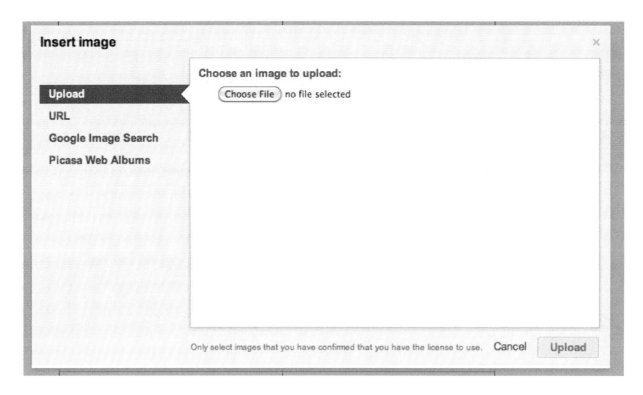

Back in the document, I clicked on the image icon and picked upload to upload the file from my desktop.

4.)

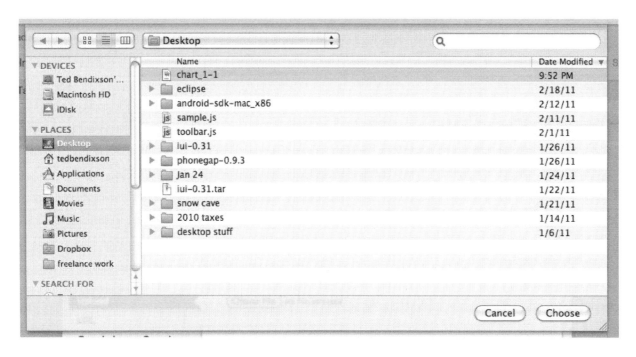

After that, the file uploads and it gets inserted into the document. You never have to worry about image file sizes when you're working with charts and graphs in Google Docs. None of the charts you generated will ever be so large as to violate Google's uploading restrictions. This is the most efficient way to go about doing this.

Functions, functions, and more functions.

Toward the end of the last section, we used two functions to calculate some important numbers, both the average taxation rate and the maximum taxation rate. But Google Spreadsheets is loaded full of functions. You can find them all in the function browser.

There are two ways to get to the function browser. You can get there by going to insert --> function --> more, or you can just click on the Sigma shape in the toolbar and pick "more formulas."

Be aware that Google spreadsheets will place the formula into the box you have selected, so you better make sure you know where you want to use your formula before you use it.

File	Edit	View	Insert	Format	Form	Tools	Help

Formula:

	A	B	C	D	
1	Year	Tax Rate			SUM
2	1995	0.01			AVERAGE
3	1996	0.05			COUNT
4	1997	0.1			MAX
5	1998	2			MIN
6	1999	5			
7	2000	5.5			More formulas…
8	2001	5.2			
9	2002	5.8			
10	2003	7			
11	2004	7.1			
12	2005	8.1			
13	2006	8.3			
14	2007	8.43			
15	2008	10			
16	2009	11.2			
17	2010	13			
18					
19	Average Tax:	6.049375		**Taxation Without Representation**	
20	Max:	13			
21	Some Function:		16		

Inside the function browser, you'll see all of the different functions separated by the category they fit into. There are functions for basic math, finances, and statistics as well as a few other Google-provided treats. If you have some free time, it's a good idea to look through these to see if any of them can help you out later on.

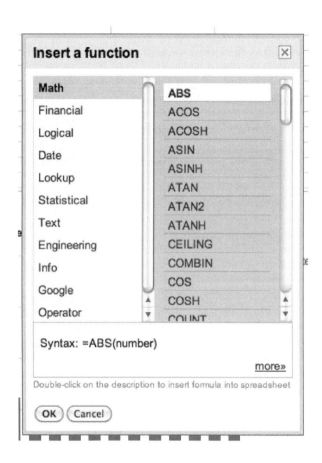

For the time being, we're going to add some more complex statistical calculations to our spreadsheet. Click on statistical and then double click on STDEV to insert it into the cell we picked earlier.

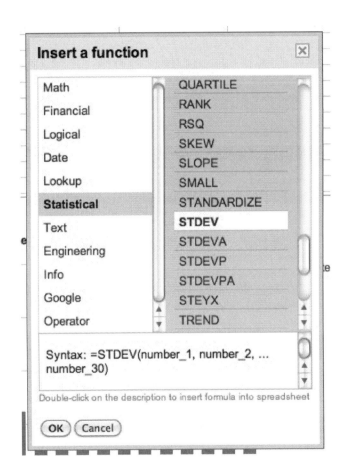

Insert a function ☒

Math	QUARTILE
Financial	RANK
Logical	RSQ
Date	SKEW
Lookup	SLOPE
Statistical	SMALL
Text	STANDARDIZE
Engineering	**STDEV**
Info	STDEVA
Google	STDEVP
Operator	STDEVPA
	STEYX
	TREND

Syntax: =STDEV(number_1, number_2, ... number_30)

Double-click on the description to insert formula into spreadsheet

(OK) (Cancel)

Now our cell will have an empty standard deviation function inside of it. Just like we did earlier, we simply need to tell Google Spreadsheets which range of values to use for the standard deviation calculation. In this case, we're going to pick the values from B2 through B17.

Formula:	=STDEV(B2:B17)	
	A	**B**
1	Year	Tax Rate
2	1995	0.01
3	1996	0.05
4	1997	0.1
5	1998	2
6	1999	5
7	2000	5.5
8	2001	5.2
9	2002	5.8
10	2003	7
11	2004	7.1
12	2005	8.1
13	2006	8.3
14	2007	8.43
15	2008	10
16	2009	11.2
17	2010	13
18		
19	Average Tax:	6.049375
20	Max:	13
21	Some Function:	=STDEV(B2:B17)
22		

Press enter, and you'll get a number around 3.91 as the standard deviation of our tax rate. We could keep going further down this rabbit hole, looking at all the different functions, but I think you get the point. Whenever you don't know which function to use, the function browser will make it a lot easier on you. Just double click and the work is done. Once you've remembered which functions you need to use, you can start typing the equals sign and Google's autocomplete will find the function for you.

Can't find a function that does what you want? Try installing a script.

Google Spreadsheets comes with a bunch of different functions, but it doesn't always have everything you need. That's where scripts can come in handy. They can take care of the calculations nobody wants to do on their own, and because they're made by Google Spreadsheet users just like you, there's a good chance that you'll find something to help you out.

Scripts can be found by going to Tools --> Scripts --> Insert. There's also a script editor that allows you to create your own scripts, but that's a little too advanced for this guide. We simply want to reap the benefit of the work others have done.

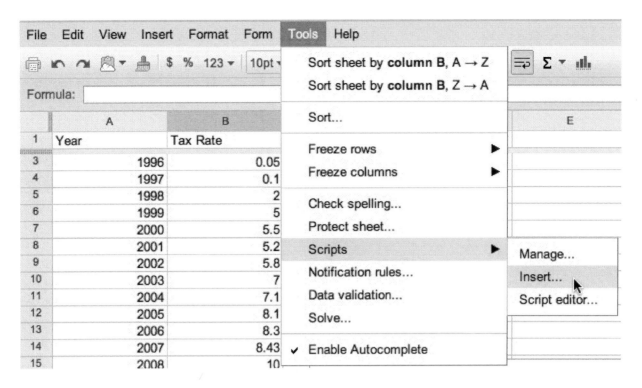

Now you'll see a giant library of the different scripts other Google Spreadsheets users have written. There are scripts for business, statistics, fun and games, and much more. Have a look around these when you get the time. There's a lot to do.

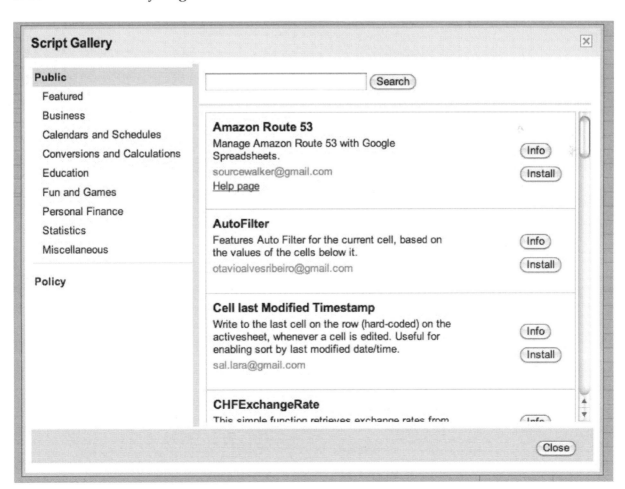

For the purpose of our project, we simply want a script that will insert today's date into a cell. There's a script called "insert today's date" that does this, so let's go ahead and use it. Click on Install.

When you click on Install, you'll be asked to authorize the script and allow it to read and write to your spreadsheet. If you're concerned about viruses, don't be. The message is merely intended to get you thinking about potentially dangerous scripts that could run havoc on your spreadsheet. As long as you use the scripts in the way they're intended to be used, you should be okay. Click authorize.

If the install was a success, you'll get a little popup window telling you that you can run the script. Nothing will happen just yet. We still need to find a cell where we want to place our script in order to use it. Let's do that.

We'll create an extra field at the bottom, and we'll call it "Date: ". Next to that field, we'll insert our script.

13	2006	8.3
14	2007	8.43
15	2008	10
16	2009	11.2
17	2010	13
18		
19	Average Tax:	6.049375
20	Max:	13
21	Some Function:	3.94832026520983
22	Date:	
23		

With cell B22 selected, let's go back to the tools menu. This time, we'll pick Tools --> Scripts --> Manage...

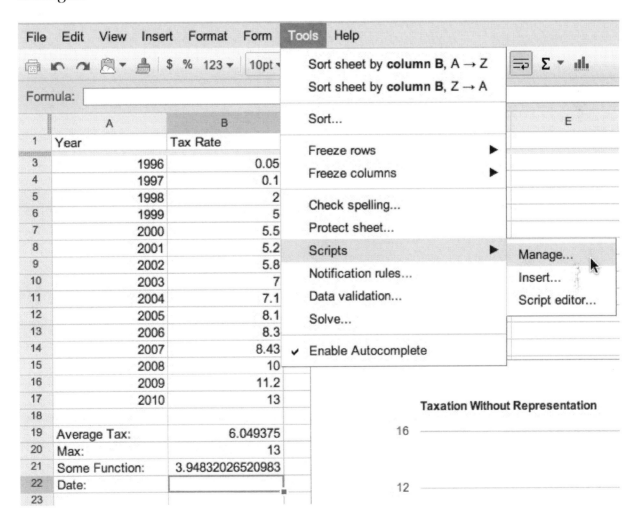

The script manager will give us a list of all the scripts we've installed on our Google Spreadsheets account. To get a script to run in the cell we've selected, we click on "run." In this case, we'll pick the first script, "insertTodaysDate" and we'll run it.

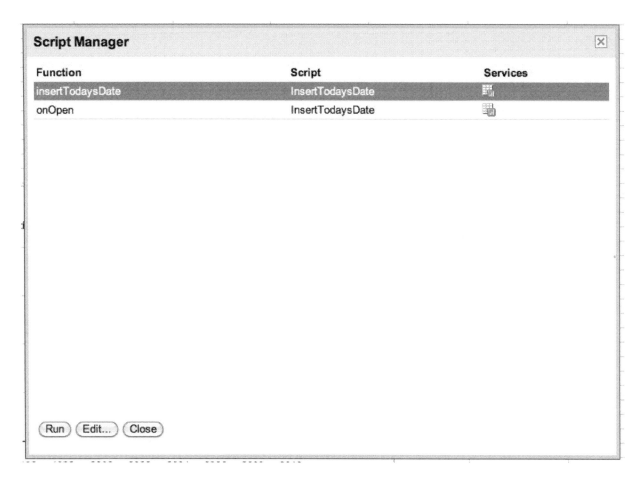

Lo and behold, today's date appears in the cell we selected earlier. Pretty cool for not having to do any coding whatsoever.

17		2010	13
18			
19	Average Tax:		6.049375
20	Max:		13
21	Some Function:		3.94832026520983
22	Date:		2/27/2011
23			
24			

Just so you know, while you have the script manager open, you can click on any other cell and run the script in it as well. This helps when you need to add a bunch of different scripts to your spreadsheet.

Go ahead and click on the cell with the date in it. A calendar should pop up. As you switch around the dates on the calendar, it changes in the date box. Who could've expected that you can do so much inside of a simple spreadsheet editor?

Average Tax:	6.049375
Max:	13
Some Function:	3.94832026520983
Date:	2/27/2011

«	**February 2011**					»
S	**M**	**T**	**W**	**T**	**F**	**S**
30	31	1	2	3	4	5
6	7	8	9	10	11	12
13	14	15	16	17	18	19
20	21	22	23	24	25	26
27	28	1	2	3	4	5
6	7	8	9	10	11	12

Managing spreadsheets and collaboration with Google Spreadsheets.

When you're the only one working on a project, it's easy to know what's causing any particular problem. But when you're working on the same spreadsheet with multiple partners, it starts to get confusing. Someone makes a change and it affects all of your data. Now nobody knows when the change took place and how you can bring your spreadsheet back to a state of sanity.

The team behind Google Spreadsheets anticipated these sorts of problems, and they built in a few safeguards. You can use notifications to stay on top of any spreadsheet changes, data validation to keep the wrong data from getting in, and protection to stop the wrong users from messing with your data.

By the way, the process of sharing spreadsheets is the same in Google Spreadsheets as it is in Google Documents. You simply click on the share button and pick the person who you want to give access to your spreadsheet. Nothing new here.

Use notifications to stay in the loop whenever a page changes.

With notifications, you'll get an email every time someone makes a change to a range of cells or a single sheet. This will definitely come in handy when it's time to diagnose a problem with your data.

To sign up for notifications, go to tools --> notification rules.

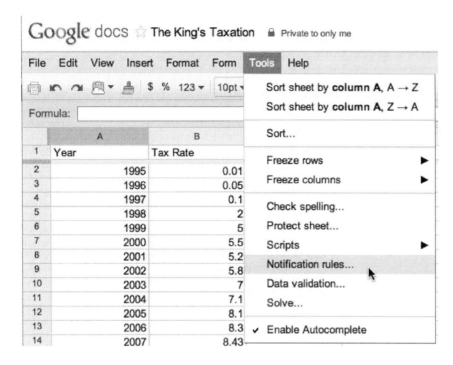

When you click on this, you'll get a dialog box with your notification options.

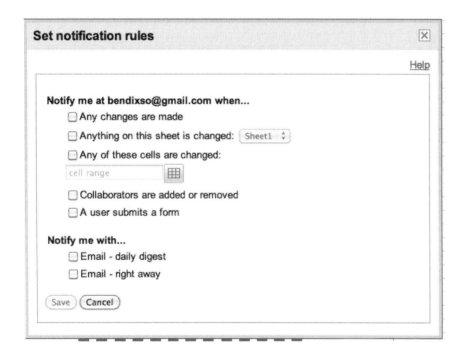

The first few options determine when you'll get notified while the last option determines how you'll get notified. If you're very serious about your data, you'll choose the last option so you can have an accurate log of changes. Otherwise, go for the daily digest.

Remember that any and all changes will be sent to your Gmail account. If you're using a different email account, you might want to consider getting your Gmail forwarded to it. I hate to say that, but there is no other way around this.

Determining who gets to edit what.

I certainly don't trust everyone. You shouldn't either. In Google Spreadsheets, you can specify who gets to edit your spreadsheet and who will have to be satisfied with viewing it. To get to these options, go to tools --> protect sheet.

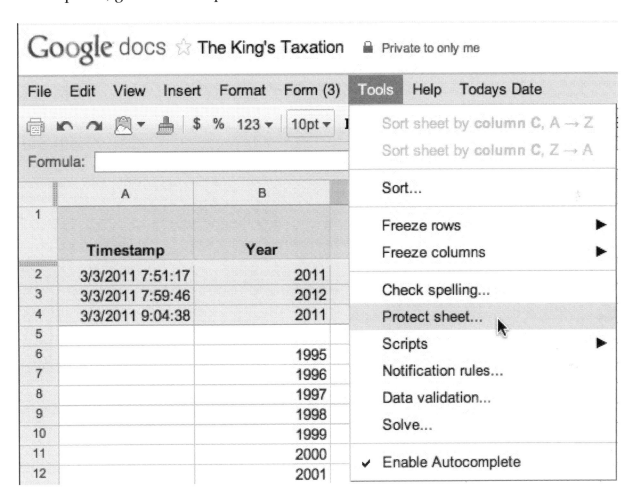

Now you'll be given a dialog box where you can give spreadsheet access to the appropriate people.

Once you invite people to collaborate, you'll be able to select them from this list. Click done, and your sheet will be protected from the collaborators who don't know what they're doing.

How to prevent data corruption from happening in the first place.

It's one thing to monitor your spreadsheet, but it's even better to ensure that none of your data gets messed up in the first place. A few simple rules and safeguards can go a long way toward preventing these mistakes from happening. That's why Google Spreadsheets features data validation.

What is data validation? Simply put, it's a set of rules you use to make sure the data going into your spreadsheet makes sense. Let's say your spreadsheet contains a bunch of phone numbers. Would it make sense for any of those numbers to have a question mark in them? Nope. Never. So why not screen out that typo with an error message so your user is forced to enter something that can pass the common sense test?

That's the basic idea behind data validation. We tell Google Spreadsheets what is and is not acceptable for certain sections of our spreadsheet, and Google Spreadsheets does the rest. When someone accidentally enters a question mark, it doesn't get entered into the spreadsheet. The user (collaborator in this case) is forced to enter something else.

Data validation can be as simple or as complex as you need or want it to be. You can use 500 rules, or you can use just one. As your spreadsheet evolves, your data validation rules evolve with it.

For now, we'll just make one rule. To get started, we'll go to tools --> data validation.

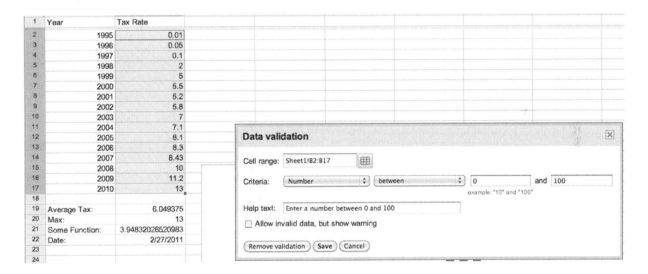

The data validation box lets you create one rule at a time for a specific set of cells.

In this case, we're going to add the common sense rule that any percentage must be a number between zero and 100. The King can tax us all he wants, but it doesn't make sense for him to tax us anything above 99%. That's simply too much.

The cell range we've picked is B2 through B17, all the tax rates we've entered so far. Our criteria is any number between zero and 100.

Once you get this far, the help text is automatically generated. You'll see this text when your mouse cursor hovers over the cell range you've specified. If your collaborators are still confused about why they can't enter data after reading your help message, then you either need a better help message or you need to fire someone. Pick your poison.

The final checkbox is for people who don't want to stop data corruption outright. If you check it, your spreadsheet will allow invalid data, but it will also display a warning message to the collaborator who tried to break the rules. Whether you want to use it depends on how you strict you are about the data that goes into your spreadsheet.

Now let's click "save." Just to test everything out, head over to one of the rows of data in column B and try to change it to a number that's greater than 100.

B
Tax Rate
0.01
0.05
0.1
2
5
5.5
5.2
5.8
107
7.1
8.1

Whenever you try and do this, the number reverts back to the old number, and your help message gets displayed very clearly. Keep this is mind because it's what will happen whenever someone else modifies your spreadsheet in an inappropriate way.

B	C	D
Tax Rate		
0.01		
0.05		
0.1		
2		
5		
5.5		
5.2		
5.8		
7	validation Enter a number	
7.1	between 0 and 100	
8.1		
8.3		
8.43		

Organizing survey data with Google Spreadsheets.

Have you ever wanted to take a simple poll at your office? With Google Spreadsheets and Google forms, it's really easy to add data to any spreadsheet using an online form. With the data in place, your spreadsheet can do all the calculating for you. Here's how to get started.

We're going to take the same taxation spreadsheet we've been working with this whole time. We won't need to do any modifications to the spreadsheet. We'll start by going to the form menu and clicking "create a form."

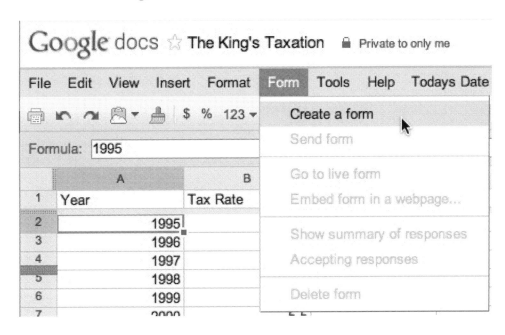

Now you'll see what looks a form created from the two columns in your spreadsheet, year and tax rate. With a few modifications, we can tell our users how to answer the questions so we can get the kind of data we want.

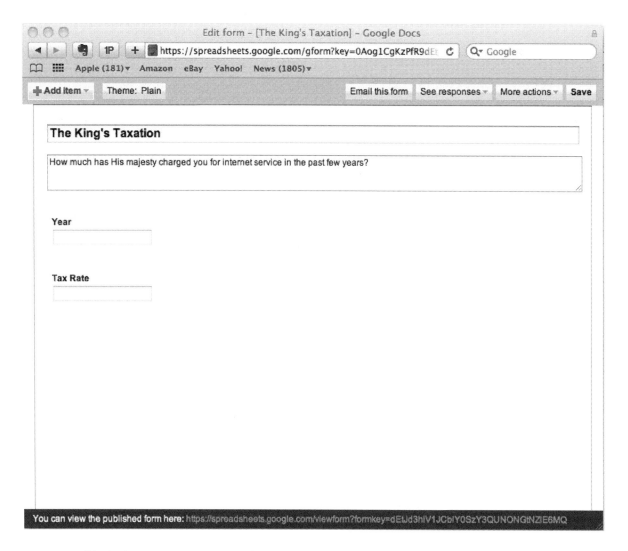

Now we'll click Save to save our form online. Let's also preview our published form by clicking on the blue link at the bottom. When we do this, here's what we get.

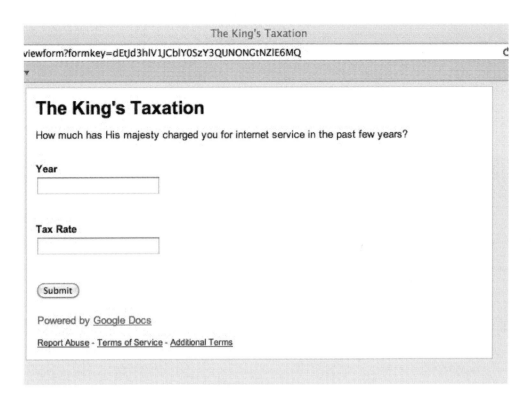

When you fill out the form, the data goes straight to your spreadsheet. You can also email this link to anyone else whose input you'd like to receive. If you add in a few data validation checks on the spreadsheet itself, you're guaranteed to get data that makes sense. This will definitely come in handy when you need to organize your numbers.

For now, let's enter one data point. Put "2011" for the year and "5" for the tax rate. Click on submit.

You'll be given a "thank you message" and the option to return to the form you just filled out. Now let's have a look at what's changed in your spreadsheet.

A	B	C
Timestamp	Year	Tax Rate
3/3/2011 7:51:17	2011	5
	1995	0.01
	1996	0.05
	1997	0.1
	1998	2
	1999	5
	2000	5.5
	2001	5.2
	2002	5.8
	2003	7
	2004	7.1
	2005	8.1
	2006	8.3
	2007	8.43
	2008	10
	2009	11.2
	2010	13
	Average Tax:	6.049375
	Max:	13
	Some Function:	3.94832026520983
	Date:	2/27/2011

Lo and behold, an entire column has been added. It contains a timestamp for the new data. Now you'll know exactly when certain user-generated changes have taken place. We've also got the exact same numbers we entered into the form. How's that for simple and easy?

What happens when your user inputs a number that violates your validation rules?
Let's say someone comes along, and being the *absolutely insane* 2012 Mayan prophecy speculator that he is, truly believes in his heart that 2012 will be the end of the Internet (and world) as we know it. He thinks the king will raise Internet taxes to 120% of the cost of Internet service. Anyone who gets Internet will have to pay the king the entire cost of his or her Internet service plus an additional 20%. Talk about apocalyptic.

Here's what he enters into our form:

The King's Taxation

How much has His majesty charged you for internet service in the past few years?

Year

2012

Tax Rate

120

(Submit)

Powered by Google Docs

Report Abuse - Terms of Service - Additional Terms

What do you think will happen when he clicks "submit?" Will his data get entered into our spreadsheet, or will we be free of his complete and utter speculation without any regard to common sense or reason? Here's what happens...

Something bad happened. Don't worry, though. The Spreadsheets Team has been notified and we'll get right on it.

Visit our help center

Google docs

Hooray for data validation! We've saved our spreadsheet from idle minds who have nothing better to do with their time than read up on fantasies of how the world will come to an end. Unfortunately, our error message isn't specific enough to let our user know he has entered a number that doesn't fit into our data validation rules.

Depending on your perspective, this is either a good or a bad thing. If you want your user to know your validation rules so she can enter the right kind of data, it's a bad thing. If you want to drive away hordes of crazy people who enjoy reading books on mystical revelation, UFOs, and remote viewing, it's a good thing.

All manner of judgment aside, it seems as though this is a feature of Google Spreadsheets that the Google team hasn't quite polished yet. You'll have to tell your users in an email, or with some text at the top of the form, that they have to pick a number between 1 and 100, or they'll get an error message. This is something to keep in mind when making surveys and forms.

A quick way to add more data to your spreadsheet.

While we're on the topic of forms and the way they fit into spreadsheets, there is a quick way to add new data to your spreadsheet. Go back to the edit form page and click on Add Item --> Questions --> Text.

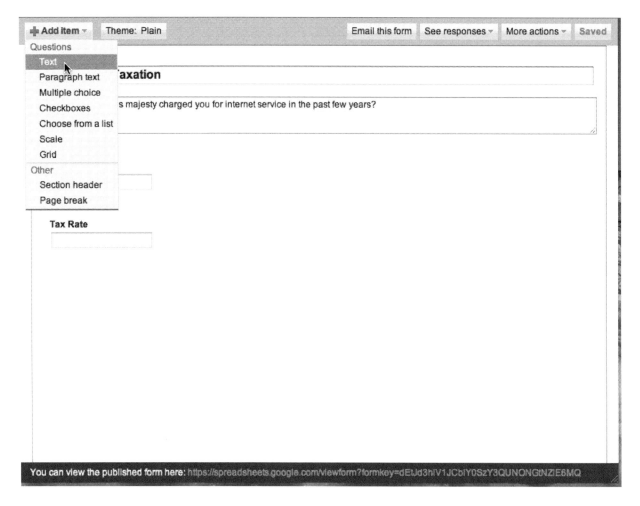

When you click on this, you'll get a text box where you can enter a question for whoever is filling out the form. In this case, we want to know each person's average yearly income.

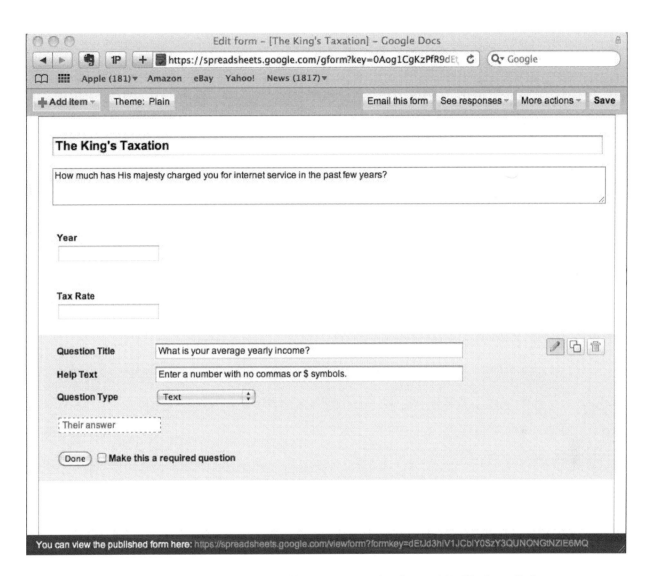

Now click done, and your question will appear on the form. We'll also click save so we can test everything out.

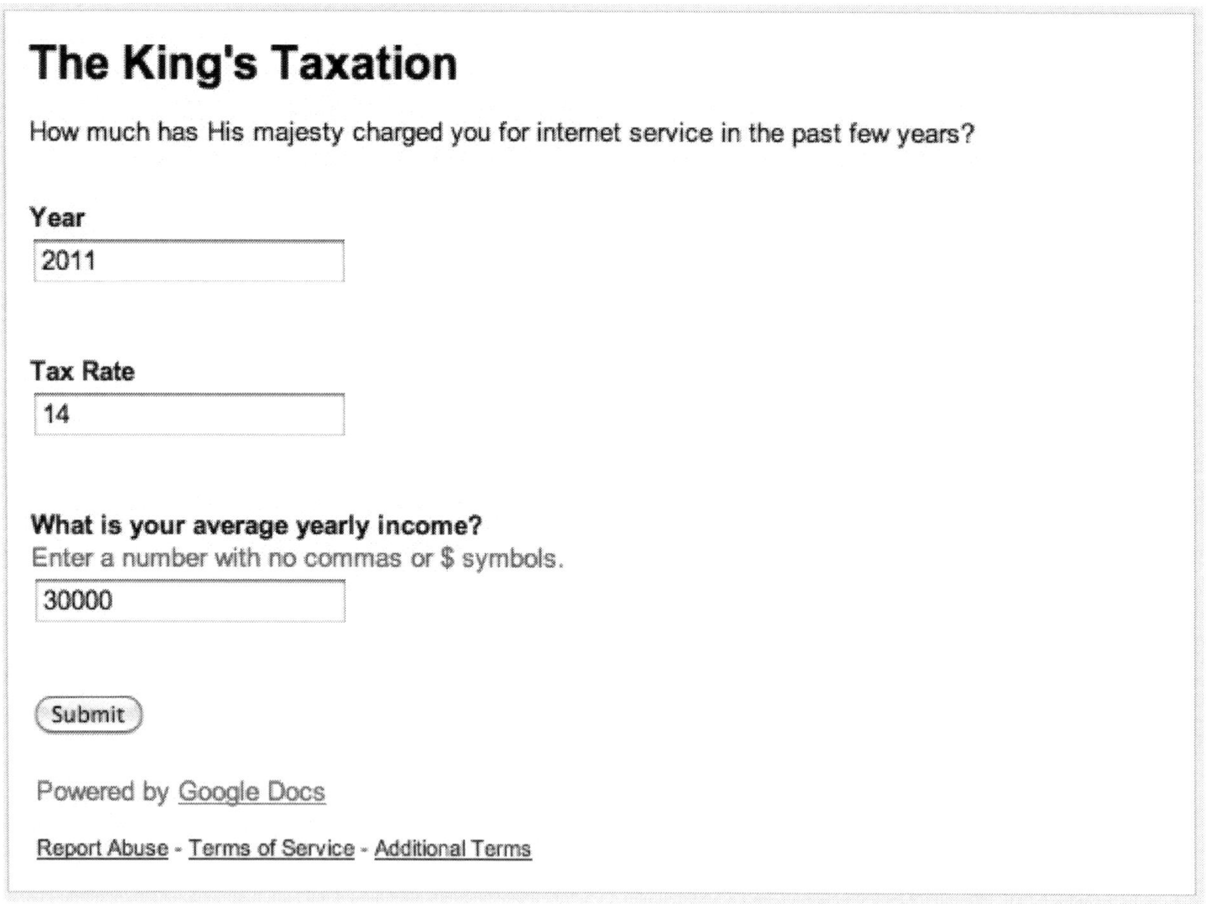

The King's Taxation

How much has His majesty charged you for internet service in the past few years?

Year

2011

Tax Rate

14

What is your average yearly income?
Enter a number with no commas or $ symbols.

30000

(Submit)

Powered by Google Docs

Report Abuse - Terms of Service - Additional Terms

The above is a snapshot of our new form, complete with the question we've added. Let's put some data into it so we can see what happens. When you've entered these numbers, click on "submit."

	A	B	C	D
1	Timestamp	Year	Tax Rate	What is your average yearly income?
2	3/3/2011 7:51:17	2011	5	
3	3/3/2011 7:59:46	2012	99	
4	3/3/2011 9:04:38	2011	14	30000
5				
6		1995	0.01	
7		1996	0.05	
8		1997	0.1	
9		1998	2	
10		1999	5	
11		2000	5.5	
12		2001	5.2	
13		2002	5.8	
14		2003	7	
15		2004	7.1	
16		2005	8.1	
17		2006	8.3	
18		2007	8.43	
19		2008	10	
20		2009	11.2	
21		2010	13	

Check it out. We've got a new data point from the question we just asked. You can keep going on and on with this, adding new kinds of data as you add questions to your form.

When we first conceived of this guide, we were going to write about Google Spreadsheets and Google Forms as if they were two separate things. However, as we continued to use both in our day-to-day business dealings, we realized that it's all connected. With a few clicks, you can turn a question/answer form into a spreadsheet or vice versa. Awesome.

That's the great thing about using online spreadsheets as opposed to spreadsheets that are stuck on your hard drive. You can get anyone involved, turning them into a true collaboration machine. It doesn't matter how you need to get the data. When you make the switch to Google Spreadsheets, it's guaranteed to be much easier.

What's next?

Now that you've got the data and the speech, why not turn it into a presentation? In the next section, we'll show you how to prepare a presentation using Google Presentations. Yes, it's just like PowerPoint except online, and there are a few other additions for the purposes of collaboration.

If you're still trying to piece together a reason why you might make the switch to Google Docs, just think of it as a more collaborative Microsoft Office. No more separate files and no more sending things back and forth. Just you working with your team on a more secure platform.

Google Presentation

How many times have you gotten together with your team to create a presentation, only to find out that you're missing a few crucial slides from one person? If there is any time where online collaboration works at its best, it's when you have to come up with a group presentation ASAP. With Google presentations, you can assemble your group, get your slides together, and give the exact same presentation from any device.

Google Presentations is meant to be a free online replacement for Microsoft PowerPoint or Apple's Keynote. You'll find that much of what you can do remains the same. Presentations are built from slides that transition into another, each containing text, pictures, data, videos, and more. If you've used these programs on your desktop machine before, you should feel right at home with Google Presentations.

So let's hop right in. To create a new presentation, you click on the "create new" button from your Google Docs account, and then click "presentation."

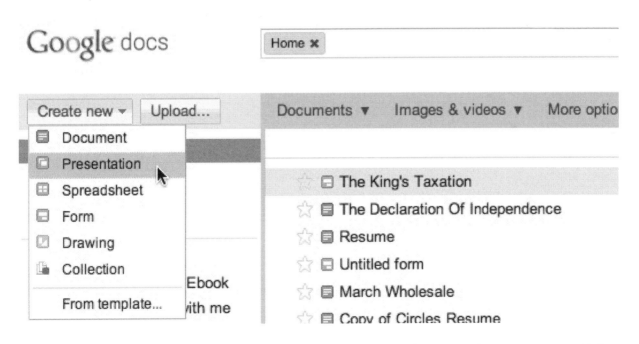

Now we'll be taken to what looks like an online version of Microsoft PowerPoint. We're already given a starting slide, but let's change it reflect what we'll be talking about.

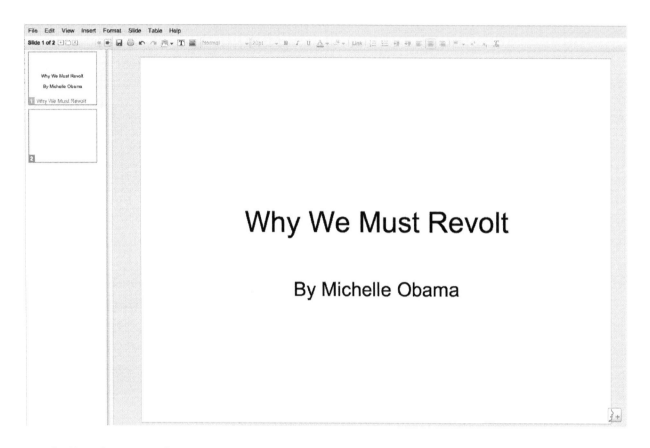

Michelle Obama is about to present her findings to the First Continental Congress. She wants to show the true reach of the King's Internet taxation and its effects on the American public.

To get this presentation off the ground, we'll create a few more slides. You can add a new slide by clicking on the + icon to the very left of the toolbar or by going to the slide menu and choosing "new slide."

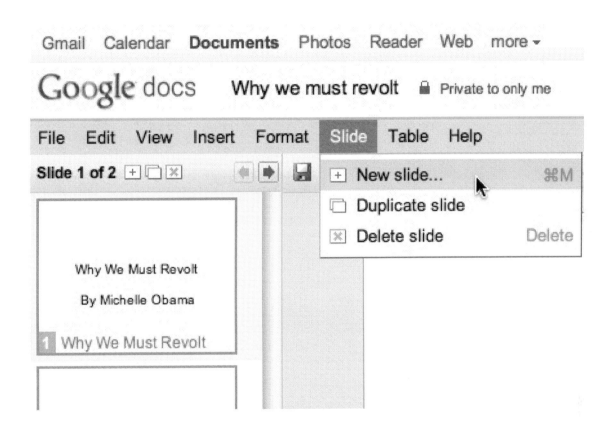

Whenever you create a new slide, you're given a few commonly used slide templates to choose from. Which one you use depends on the kind of data you need to present. Do you want to include a few talking points, or do you want to show a video? Each template serves a purpose.

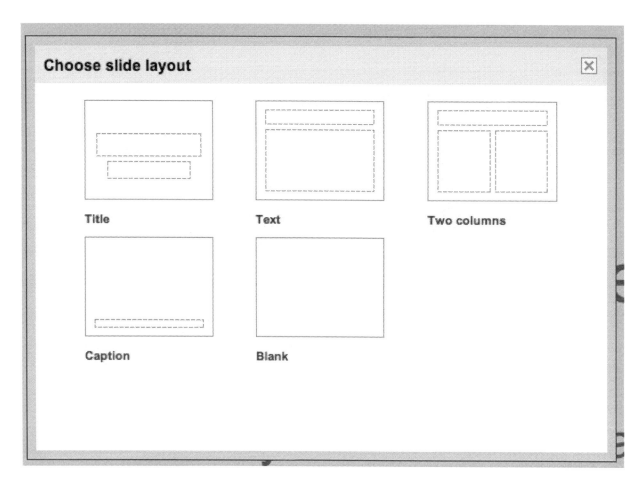

For the purpose of this exercise, we'll pick the text template. We want to illustrate all of the King's wrongdoings to the American people.

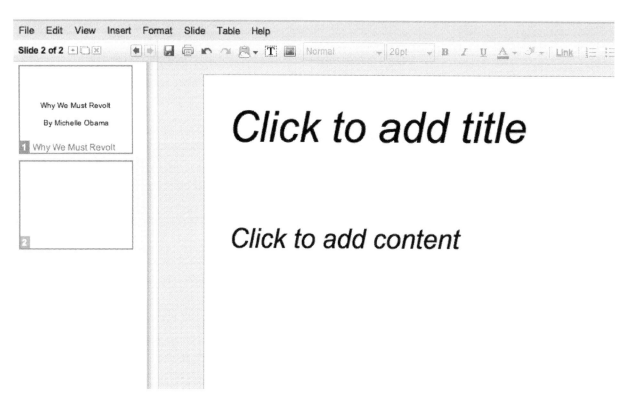

This slide is just like the title slide, but the text fields are in a different place. Let's give it a title, and let's add a few of the King's infractions from our Declaration Of Independence document.

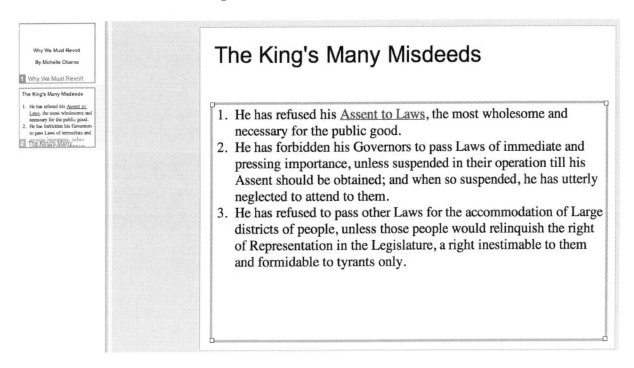

To get the bulleted numbers, you need to click on the numbered list formatting option in the toolbar. It looks like this:

Cool. We've created our first real slide. What else can we do?

Importing charts from Google Spreadsheets.

Remember the taxation chart we created in Google Spreadsheets? We're going to include it in our presentation as well. The number one reason for revolt is high Internet taxes, so Michelle really needs to bring this point home with some data. Here's how she'll do it.

Start off by creating a new slide, this time choosing the "caption" slide template. Our caption will reflect what we used in our spreadsheet, but you can be as creative as you want. I'm calling the graph "taxation without representation."

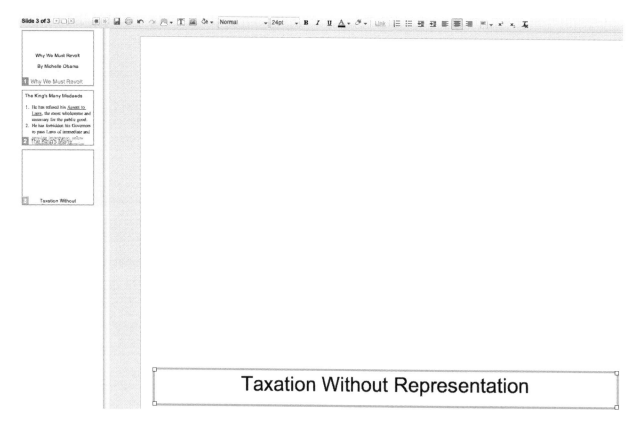

Now that you've entered a caption, go ahead and open up Google Spreadsheets. We're about to do the exact same thing we did when we inserted the chart into our Google Doc. Save the chart as an image on your hard drive, and then upload it into your presentation.

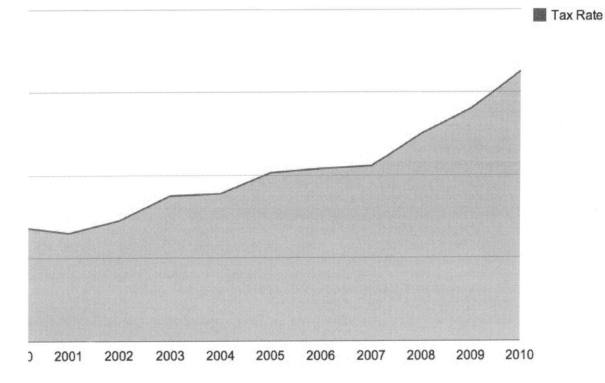

My images always save to my downloads folder, so that's where I'll grab the chart when I upload it into the presentation.

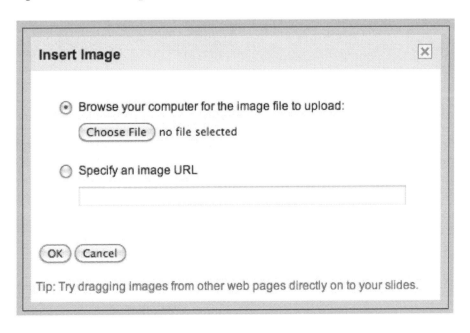

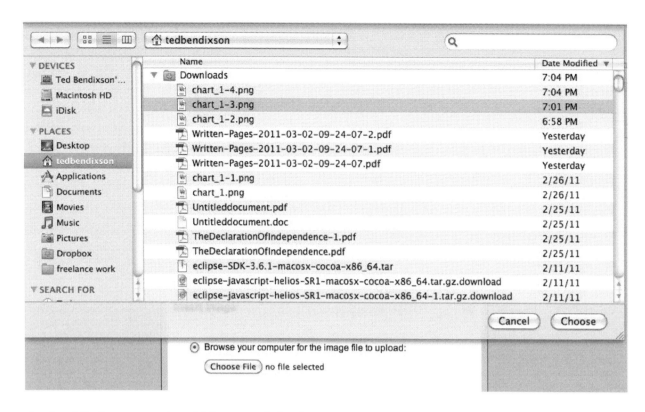

And with that, you should have a slide that contains your chart along with the caption. Pretty easy, eh?

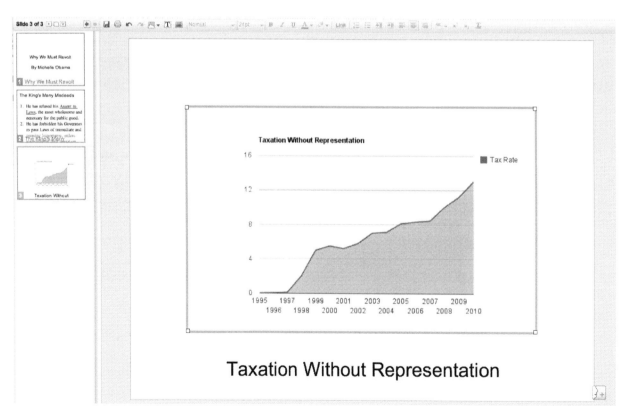

Our presentation is coming together pretty fast, but Michelle knows she isn't the same brilliant public speaker that she married. She needs to remind herself to point out a few things while she is giving her presentation. That's where speaker notes come in handy.

How to use speaker notes to remember what to say.

Do you see the little face icon with a plus symbol next to it at the bottom of the slide? Oh, you don't? Well, allow me to enlarge it.

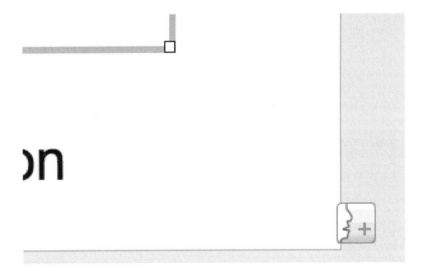

That icon gives you access to your speaker notes. When you give a presentation with Google Presentations, your speaker notes are the words that only you see. If you need to remind yourself to make a point, this is where you'll do it. Let's click on the face to learn more.

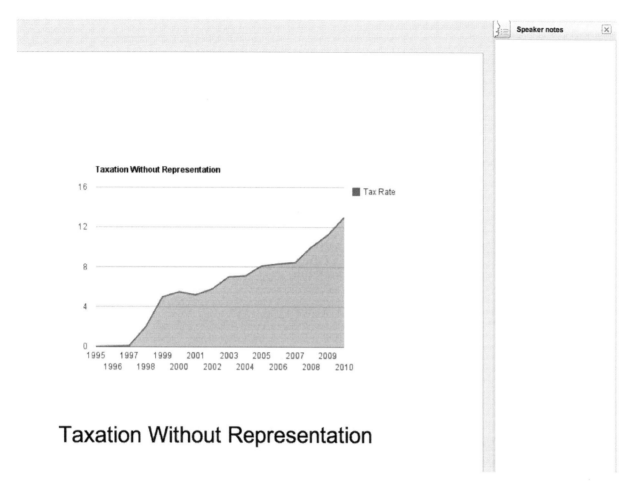

Taxation Without Representation

The sidebar on the right is for entering your notes. I've entered a few notes just to test everything out.

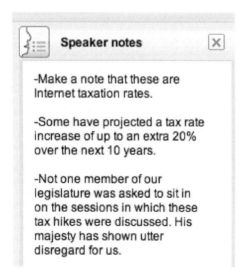

O.K. This feature is pretty cool, but how do you put it to use when you give your presentation? To see how speaker notes work in the field, we'll need to run our presentation in full screen mode.

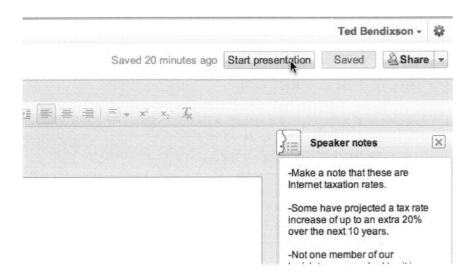

Right next to the share button, you'll find a button that says, "start presentation." When you click on it, your presentation will begin.

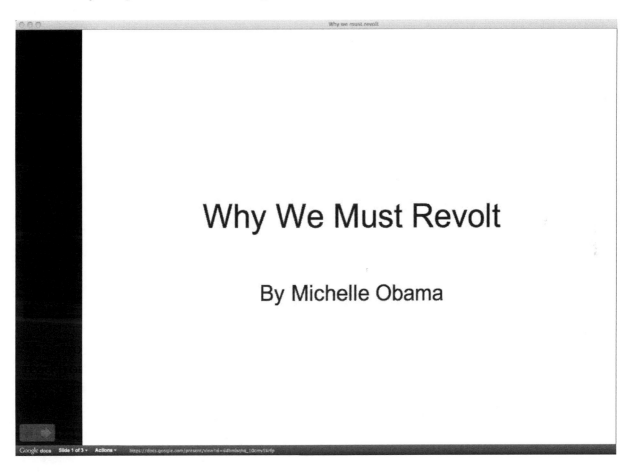

The arrows on the left will step you through the slides as you present. It's a little difficult to read from this screenshot, but there is an "actions" menu at the bottom. Let's blow it up so you can see it more clearly.

Under actions, you'll find a bunch of options that will help you out when you're in the heat of giving your presentation. For now, we're going to click on "show speaker notes."

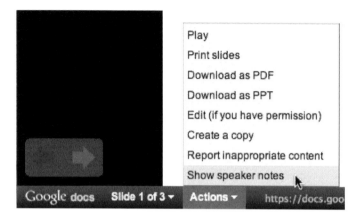

When you do this, a tiny window with the notes for the current slide will pop up. As you are aware, we never entered any notes for the first or second slides, so we'll need to go to the third slide before we start to see anything.

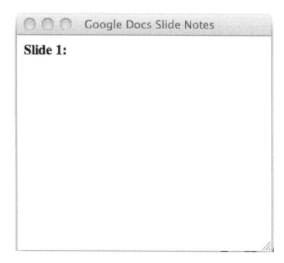

The window for your slide notes is small for a reason. When you hook up a projector and give your presentation, you're supposed to move the slide notes window to your laptop screen so it's out of view of your audience. That way, you can glance over at your notes every now and again to remember which points you need to address.

Slide 3:

-Make a note that these are Internet taxation rates.

-Some have projected a tax rate increase of up to an extra 20% over the next 10 years.

-Not one member of our legislature was asked to sit in on the sessions in which these tax hikes were discussed. His majesty has shown utter disregard for us.

How to share your presentation with others.

If you haven't noticed it already, you are viewing a public version of your presentation. The link to the right of the actions menu goes straight to your presentation, and you can share it with everyone you know. You'll also find a few more options for those who are less inclined to using Google Presentations. Under the actions menu, your viewers can download your presentation as PowerPoint or PDF file, and they can print the slides for distribution to a classroom.

And this brings me to another point. Always, always, always download every Google Presentation you make as a PowerPoint presentation, just in case you lose Internet service when you're supposed to present. Nothing is more embarrassing than explaining that the reason you can't give your presentation is because it's stored on the Internet, and the Internet is down. Nobody likes it when you waste their time.

Giving your presentation from a smartphone or tablet device.

Maybe you're in a meeting or you're having a quick conversation with someone you just met. One of the cool things about Google Presentations is the ability to show them to anyone from any device. You might have your phone with your, or maybe you brought your iPad. To get to your presentation, just go to your Google Docs account and open it up.

I brought out my iPad for this demo. Here's a quick snapshot of my Google Docs account from my iPad.

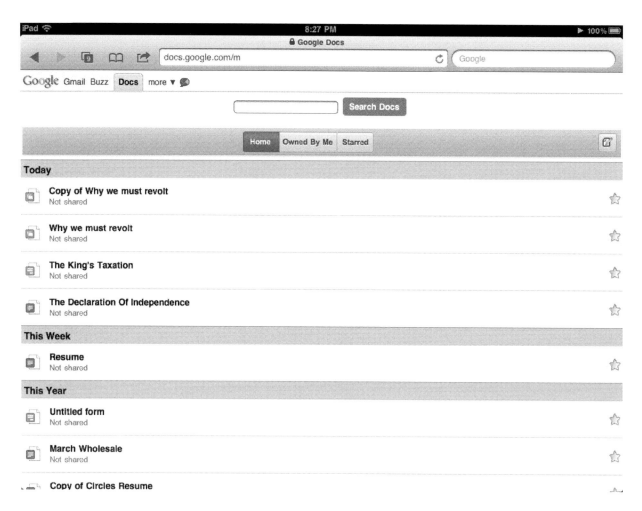

To get to my presentation, I simply tap on "why we must revolt" under today's items. Just as you could expect, my presentation loads in full screen mode. Check it out.

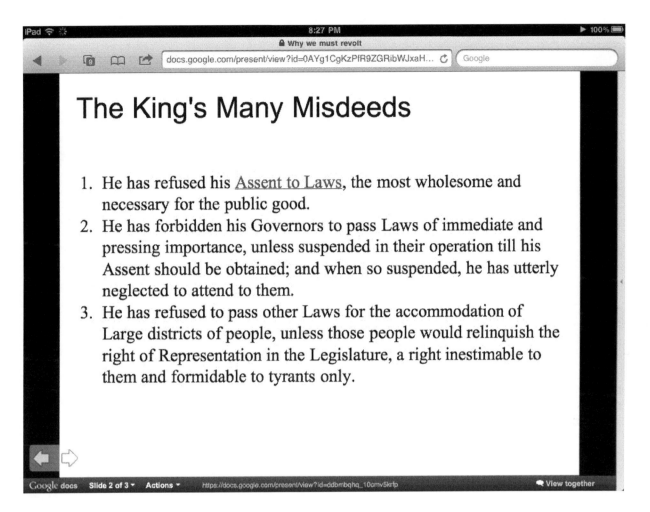

From here, you could hook up your smartphone/tablet to a projector and get started, or you could hand your device over to your friend. Just remember that if you are going to use your iPad, iPhone, or other portable device to display your presentation publicly, you should always have a backup plan in case the internet goes down. Maybe your iPhone gets 3G. That would be a good backup plan.

Adding video to your presentation.

Video is the icing on the cake and usually the most enjoyable part of any presentation. Adding video is fairly easy in Google Presentations, but it doesn't work in the way you might expect. Unfortunately, Google Docs doesn't allow you to upload your own videos directly to your presentation. You need to use your YouTube account to do that. Once you upload your videos to YouTube, you can then use them in your Presentation. Let's have a look at how it works.

To start, we'll create another caption slide. I called mine "The Colonies Are Falling Off A Precipice."

Once that's done, we'll go to insert --> video to open up the add video box.

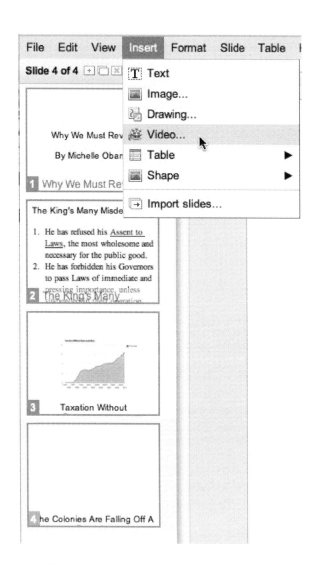

You'll probably notice a bunch of other familiar things from Google Documents. Text, images, and tables all function the same way they do in Google Documents, so I don't really feel the need to teach you anything about those. In any case, this is what our video dialog box looks like.

Just in case you were curious, all of these are YouTube videos. The only way to get a video you've recorded into your Google Presentation is to upload it to YouTube. This is all a part of Google's plan to get you to use as many Google products as possible. Call it what you will. At least they're giving you the software for free.

None of the videos suggested fit into our criteria. It would be nice to have something representing a precipitous fall off a cliff. Now that I recall it, there's a crazy video of this skier falling off a cliff in Austria. Let's search for "skier falls off cliff GoPro HD."

The first video is the one. Click on it and then click "select video" to add it to our presentation. And if you haven't seen this yet, you might want to drop everything you're doing right now. This guy got very lucky.

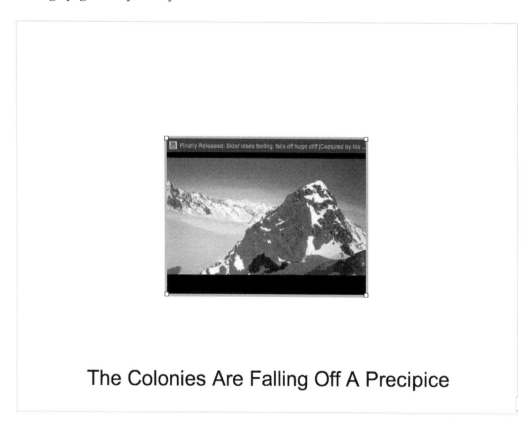

The Colonies Are Falling Off A Precipice

You can resize the video file if you want, but it's probably not necessary. YouTube features a full screen mode that you can access by clicking on the icon in the lower right hand corner of the video.

How to add your own recorded videos to your Google presentations.

All you need is a YouTube account to get started, so go to www.YouTube.com, to setup your account.

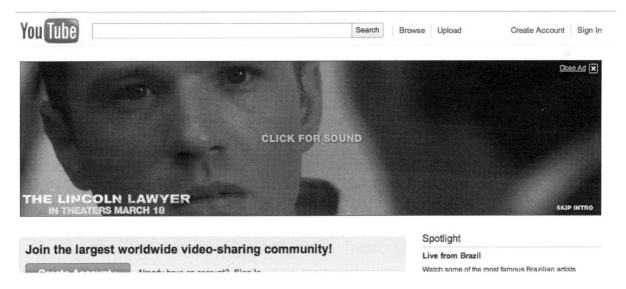

The link to create an account is in the upper right hand corner of the page. Because Google owns YouTube, it's really easy to setup an account. You can either create an account from scratch by clicking "create account," or you can use your Google Account by clicking on "sign in."

Get started with your account

Email Address: [   ]

Username: [   ]

Your username can only contain letters A-Z or numbers 0-9

Check Availability

Location: [United States   ▲▼]

Postal Code: [   ]

Date of Birth: [--- ▲▼] [--- ▲▼] [--- ▲▼]

Gender: ○ Male ○ Female

☑ Let others find my channel on YouTube if they have my email address

☐ I would like to receive occasional product-related email communications that YouTube believes would be of interest to me

Terms of Use: Please review the Google Terms of Service and YouTube Terms of Use below:

> Terms of Service
>
> 1. Your Acceptance

Uploading materials that you do not own is a copyright violation and against the law. If you upload material you do not own, your account will be deleted.

By clicking 'I accept' below you are agreeing to the YouTube Terms of Use, Google Terms of Service and Privacy Policy.

[I accept]

Option 1: Create an account from scratch.

Option 2: Leverage your Google Account

If you choose option 2, just enter your Google Account password, and you're all set. Now we just need to upload a video.

| | Search | Browse | Upload | | shredbots ▼ | Sign Out |

The upload link is at the top of YouTube's main page, right next to the browse. Click on it, and you'll be taken to the YouTube uploader.

Video File Upload

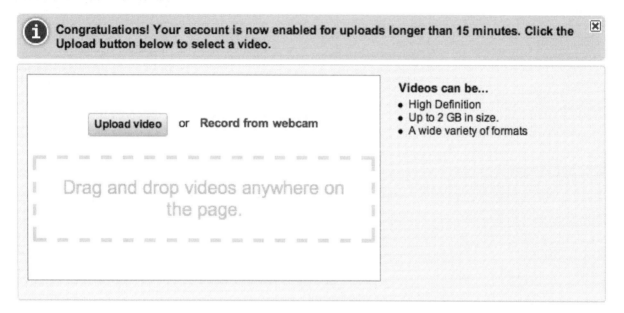

YouTube has undergone quite a few advances since we last used it. To upload your video, you can either click on the "upload video" box, or you can simply drag your video file into the dashed box. I personally prefer the latter because I can keep my videos open on my desktop to make sure I've got the right one before I upload it.

GOPR1322.MP4 (23.27M)

Upload progress: ▓▓▓ **19%** cancel
Less than a minute remaining...

Preview:

Video information and privacy settings ⌃

Title: GOPR1322.MP4

Description:

Tags:

Category: -- Select a category -- ⇕

Privacy: ⊙ Public (anyone can search for and view - recommended)
○ Unlisted (anyone with the link can view) Learn more
○ Private (only specific YouTube users can view)

Save changes   or   Skip for now

Sharing options

URL:

Embed:

While your video is uploading, you might as well change the title and add a description. To embed your video into your presentation, you simply need to search for the words in the title. It will then appear as the first result, and the rest is easy.

Back to the basics. How to use arrows and shapes to illustrate your point.

One key feature of PowerPoint and Keynote is the ability to draw shapes to convey a point. Google Presentations doesn't fall short on this category at all. From the insert menu bar, you can add arrows, circles, and boxes, or you can create your own illustrations. Let's learn how.

The next slide is meant to represent the thought process that led Michelle Obama to the conclusion that an American revolution is inevitable. Let's create it by making a new slide with the text template.

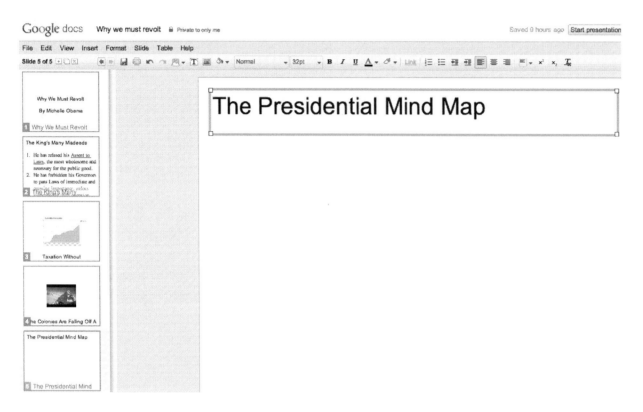

Go ahead and get rid of the second text box. We're going to use the space for our thought bubbles. To do that, move your mouse cursor over the edge of the text box and right click on it when the cursor switches to a multi-directional arrow. The delete option can be found in the menu that pops up.

Okay, let's start off with some basic thought bubbles. To add in some circles, we'll go to the insert menu, then shape, and we'll pick the bubble we want in our presentation.

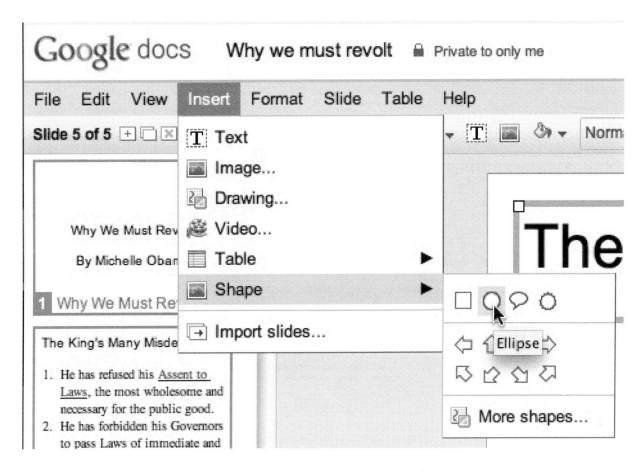

For now, let's make three bubbles, a few arrows, and some text boxes.

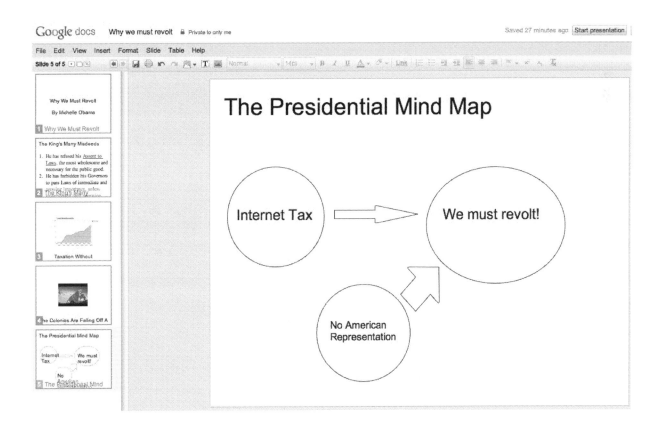

Just like in PowerPoint, you can adjust the size of the bubbles by clicking and dragging on the corners. If you hold down the shift key while you're resizing a bubble, the shape will scale proportionally.

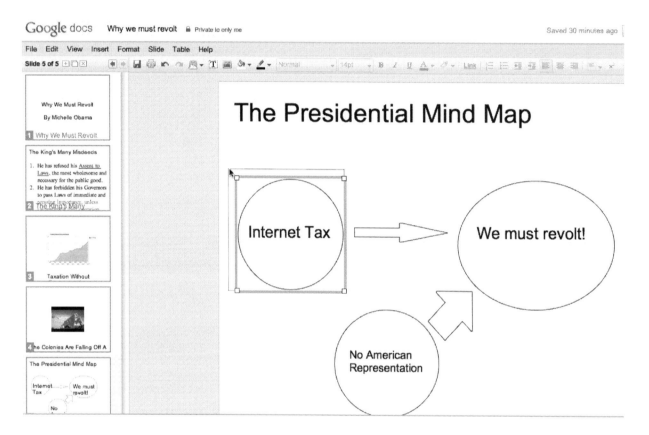

You can also move text boxes, bubbles, and shapes on the canvas by moving the mouse cursor to the edge of the shape, waiting until you see a multi-directional arrow, holding your mouse button down, and dragging.

If you want to select an entire group of objects, say, the Internet Tax bubble and the arrow next to it, hold down your left mouse button as you drag from one corner to the next, creating a selection box over the items.

146

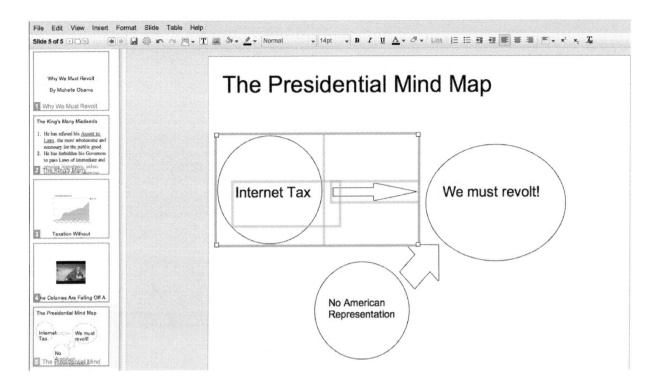

Now you can move both of these as a unit by clicking and dragging anywhere on the gray borders.

Creating your own shapes with Google Drawings.

Sometimes you'll need to create something that's a little more unique to the job you're doing. That's where Google Drawings can come in handy. We'll do an entire tutorial on Google Drawings in the next section, but for now, we'll show you how to insert a Google Drawing into your presentation.

Go to the insert menu and select drawing.

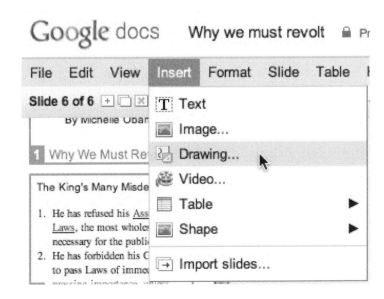

Google drawings will open up, and you can start right away. Google drawings includes a bunch of different drawing tools to make flow charts and simple graphics really easy. For now, we're going to use the line tool to write a popular slogan in red. You can find the line tool next to the arrow and shape tools.

The line tool lets you draw one line at a time. You can then use the color and thickness controls on the right to get something closer to what you want.

The control on the far left handles the color, the one next to it the thickness, and the other ones deal with creating dashed lines and other effects. I suggest you take some time to play around with these, just to see what you can do.

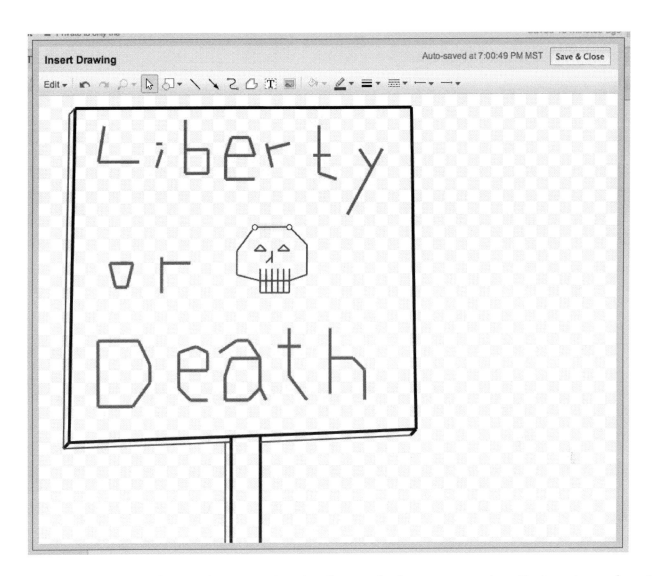

As you can see, we've made a nice sign for the revolutionary campaign. To insert our drawing into the slideshow, we need only click on the "save and close" button in the upper right hand corner. Let's do that.

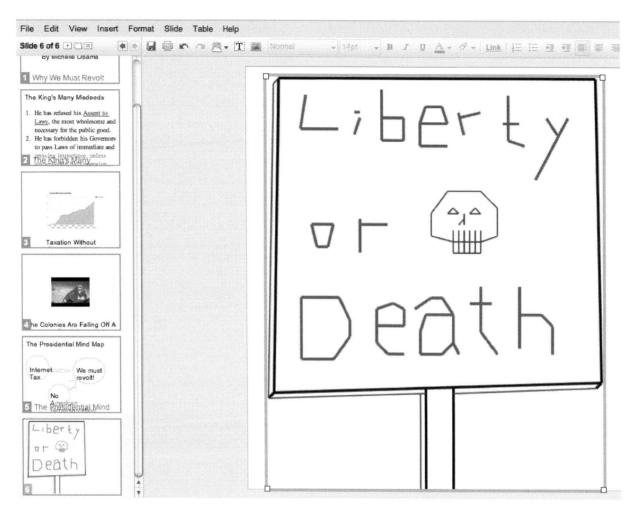

Nice. In general, I've found it's best to use Google drawings for most of your flow charts and other graphics you intend to include in your presentation. The shapes that come with Google Presentations just aren't robust enough to handle some of the more complex things you'll want to do. I found it difficult to resize and organize the shapes to create something I could actually use in a presentation.

Custom presentation templates and you.

Just like Keynote and PowerPoint, Google Presentations comes with a wide variety of presentation templates to help you out with the design side of things. It's for those who don't like to design from scratch but still want something that's visually appealing.

To test these out, we're going to leave our current (although quite lovely) slideshow behind. Let's create a new presentation by going to file --> new presentation.

By now, you should have a blank presentation to modify. To change our theme, we'll go to format --> presentation settings --> change theme.

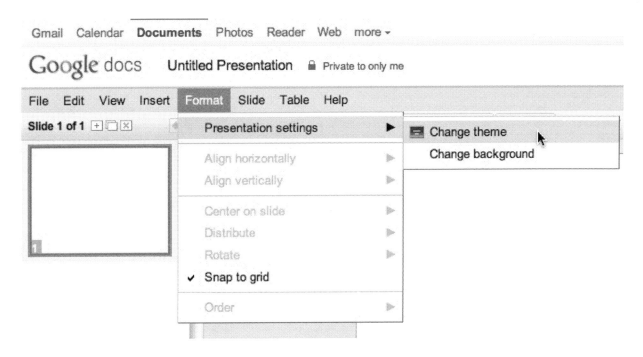

Now you'll be presented with all of the different theme options. Let's see what happens when we pick the chalkboard theme.

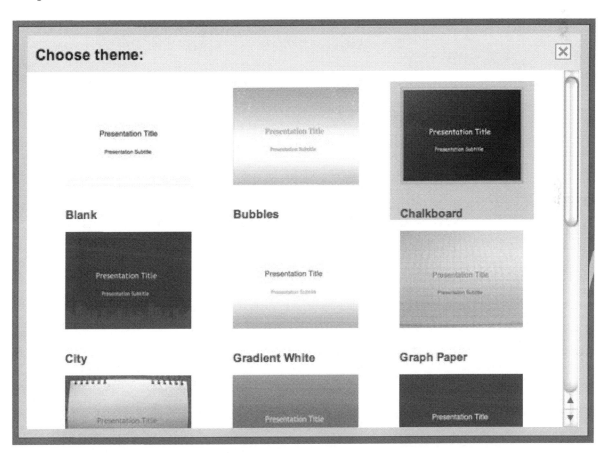

Your first slide will be switched over to the chalkboard theme, and any new slides you create will have the exact same theme. With themes, you can very quickly change the entire look and feel of your presentation.

Here's our presentation in chalkboard mode...

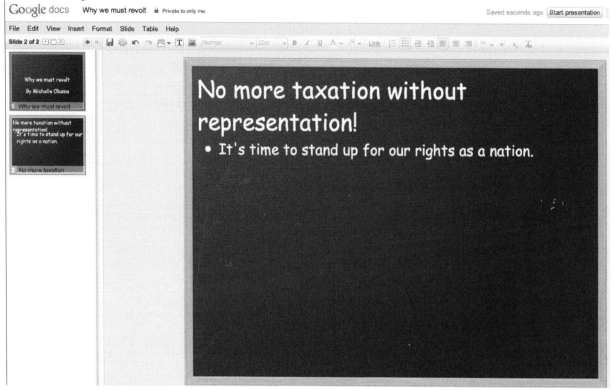

And here's the same presentation in gradient white mode...

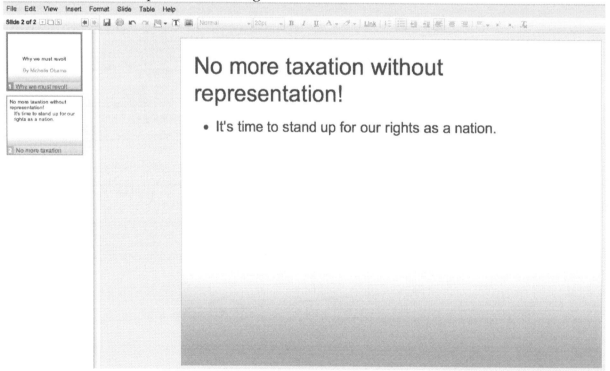

How to create a template-based presentation.

You can also download pre-made presentation templates from the web. We've tried a few these before when we were working with Google Docs, so this process should be familiar. In any case, it could come in handy if you don't want to create certain kinds of presentations from scratch. There's a good chance that someone else had to do it before, and that person may have uploaded a template to Google Docs.

To create a presentation from a template, go to the file --> new --> from template.

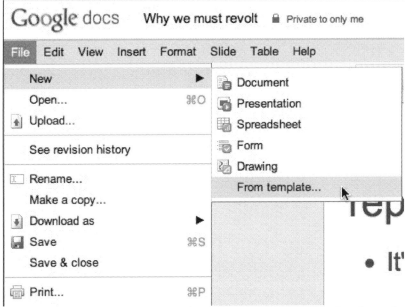

Just like before, you'll be taken to a webpage with a bunch of templates uploaded by Google Docs users who were once where you are. Admittedly, most of these templates are total junk, but if you do a careful enough search, there's a decent chance that you'll find something useful.

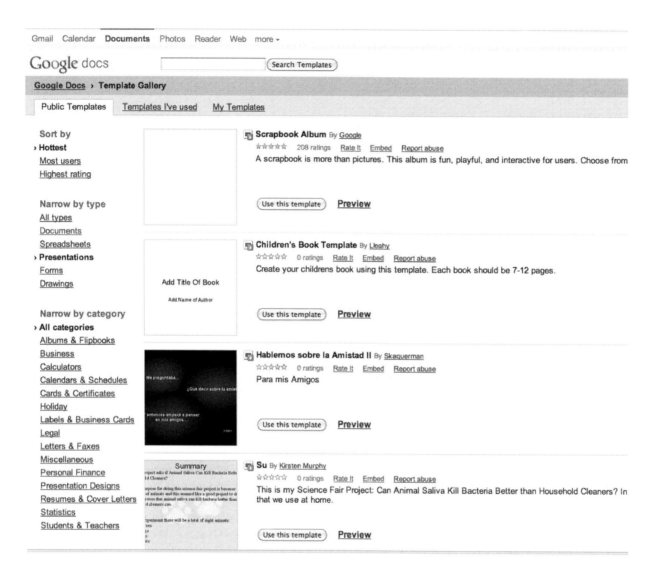

Let's try searching for a good photography presentation template. Just type "photography" into the search bar and see what comes up.

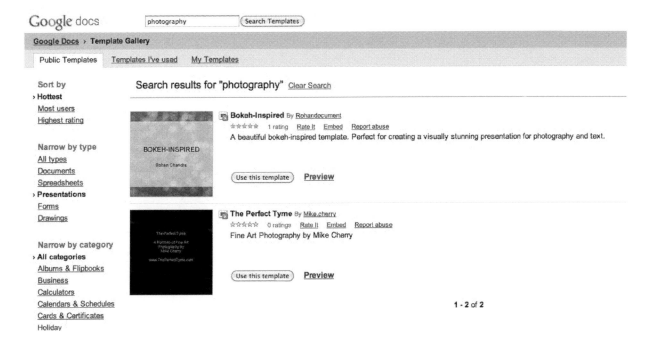

The first template looks pretty good. At least, it looks a lot more professional than most of the other ones on the site. Let's have a look through it first by clicking on the preview link to the right of the "use this template" button.

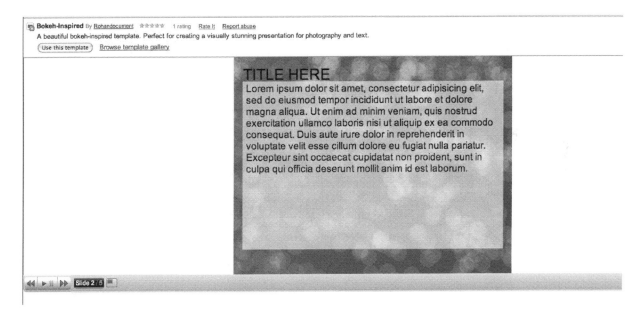

If you click through each slide, you'll see what the different slide templates look like. The person who created this template obviously put some thought into it. This template isn't exactly *my* style, but I'm sure there's someone out there who could use it.

With all these custom templates, there really is no reason to reinvent the wheel when you're building a presentation. At the very least, have a look through a few of these before you decide to get started. Maybe you can make a few simple modifications to one of them, claim it as your own, and move on.

A few more things before we leave you to fend for yourself.

Google Presentations functions much like Google Docs and Google Spreadsheets. If you understand how to print, save, and download backups of your files, you'll be setup to do the same with Google Presentations. Remember that, whenever you print, you are actually downloading your presentation to a PDF file that you then have to print later on.

We have covered almost everything there is to cover with Google Presentations. There's just one more feature we haven't touched on yet, and that is the ability to import slides from previous presentations. As it turns out, this can be a pretty useful tool when you're collaborating with others. It allows you to delegate a section of the presentation to each member of your team so you can bring it all together later on.

To import a slide from another presentation, go to insert --> import slides.

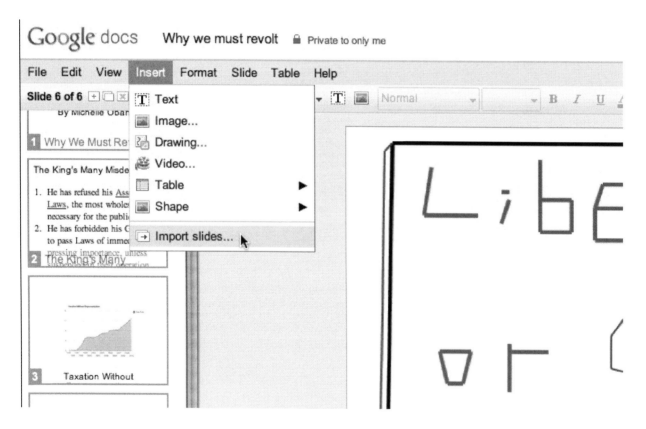

Google Docs allows you to import slides either from a Google Presentation or from a PowerPoint or Keynote file on your hard drive. For now, we'll stick with the other presentation we made.

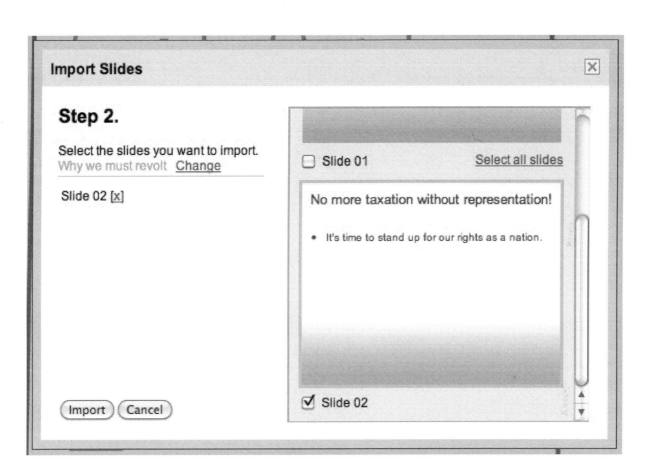

Click "import," and the next slide will be the slide from our other presentation.

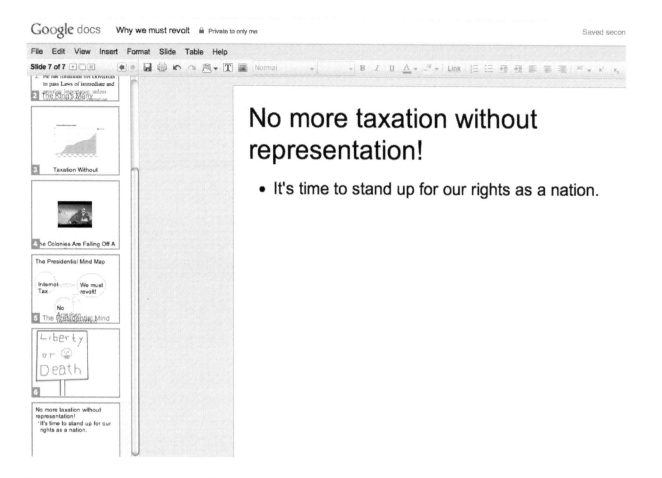

Do you notice anything different about this slide? Yep. You guessed it. This slide no longer has the gray/white gradient. It's been switched over to a plain white because that's the current theme we're using for the "Why we must revolt" presentation. Google Presentations pays attention to these kinds of things. No one slide is wedded to the presentation in which it originated. I don't see a shiny ring. Do you?

When you have a bunch of people collaborating on a presentation, this feature is amazing. You can import entire chunks of presentations all at once, and everything fits into a cohesive theme. Add in some speaker notes, and you're ready to present to the board of directors (or your high school Algebra class, either way).

Google Presentations and the Google Docs online software suite.

By now, it should be very clear how connected everything is when you're using Google Docs. Because you can easily import work from spreadsheets, drawings, forms, and docs, you can throw presentations together quite quickly. The only drawback, of course, is what happens in the off chance that the Internet goes down when you're trying to present. To prevent any consequences, always be sure to backup your presentations to a PowerPoint or PDF file.

That also wraps up our discussion of Google's Big Three. You now know how to work with Google Docs, Google Spreadsheets, and Google Presentations. The rest is details, but we'll still go through them anyway. In the next section, you'll learn a little bit more about Google drawings. With a better understanding of Google drawings, you can create more professional looking diagrams for your presentations and documents.

Google Drawing

We spent a bit of the last section discussing Google Drawings in the context of creating a presentation. In this short section, we'll go into Google Drawings with a little more detail. There are a lot of tools you can use in Google Drawings to get a graphic that's just right. And if you can't get that, you can at least get a graphic that conveys the point you're trying to make. Here a few more things you can do with Google Drawings.

Use pre-defined symbols to make a flowchart.

Google Drawings features many more symbols and graphics than the ones available in Google Presentations. There's even a set of different flowchart graphics, which definitely come in handy for presentations or other technical writing. Right now, we're going to use Google Drawings to make a flowchart that will help people determine whether the person they've just met happens to be the 80's pop sensation, Rick Astley (better known for his unforgettable hit "Never Gonna Give You Up").

To get started, we'll create a new Google Drawing from the main Google Documents menu.

To access the flowchart shapes, we'll click on the shapes button. You can find this next to the select arrow and the line tool.

You can see that Google has given the flowchart graphics their own section. There are graphics for processes, decisions, alternate decisions, and everything else you're familiar with. Thankfully, when it comes to figuring out whether we've just met Rick Astley, we only need to use a few of these shapes. Let's start out with a terminator.

When you click on the shape, the mouse cursor changes, and if you click and drag, you'll see the shape getting drawn on the screen. Here's what our first shape looks like:

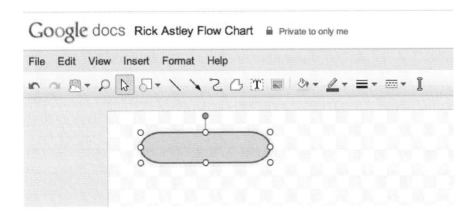

If you click and drag the dots on the corners, you'll resize the shape. If you click and drag on the green dot, you'll rotate the shape. Just for fun, let's rotate the shape 45 degrees.

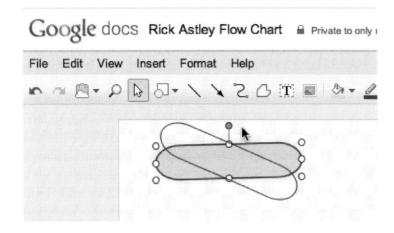

Of course, we don't need to rotate the shape for the purposes of making a flowchart. I just wanted to show you that it's possible. Move it back to its original orientation by holding down control and pressing the "z" key.

Are you ready for another side comment? Good. The best way to correct any error in Google Drawings is to hold down control and press z (ctrl + z). Those who are more perceptive will have already noticed that Google Drawings doesn't have an eraser tool. Ctrl-z basically takes you one step backwards. You can keep pressing it by the way, and each time, you'll go back another step.

Alright. Back to the flow chart. Let's give our first bubble some text. Click on the text tool to the left of the image tool.

With the text tool selected, click on your shape and type in the following, "Is he gonna?" (trust me, it will make sense later).

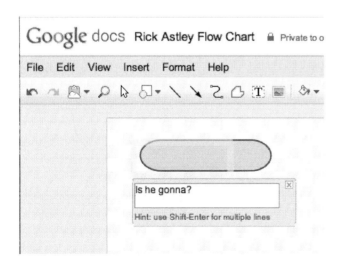

Now press enter, and your text will appear. Remember that, just like all of the other shapes in Google Drawings, you can move the text around whenever the multidirectional arrow appears. I moved mine to the center so it's nice and clean. You'll know you've hit the center when a red dashed crosshair appears.

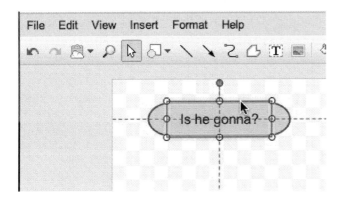

Cool. Now it's time for a decision box, which is a diamond shape. Find it in the shapes menu and add it to your flowchart.

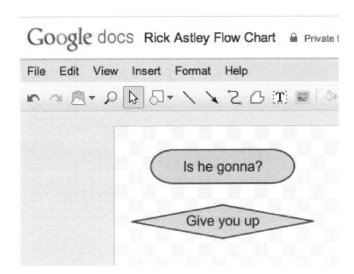

You already know how to get the text to align to the shape that contains it, but did you know you can also get the entire diamond shape to line up with the first "terminator" shape? It's easy. Just select the diamond and the text box by clicking and dragging a selection box over them, and then move them until you see a vertical red dashed line.

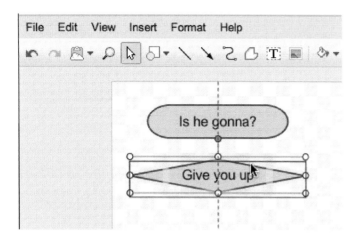

Now we're going to add a line to connect the two boxes. You're already familiar with lines from the last chapter, but there are a few cool things you can do with them when Google Drawings knows you're making a flow chart. Click on the line tool and bring your mouse cursor near the bottom of the first shape you created.

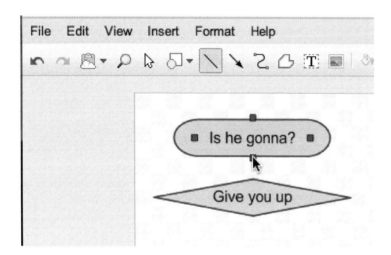

If you click on the red dot, hold your mouse button down, and then drag your cursor toward the second box until you see another red dot at the top of that box, you'll connect the two boxes with a line. It's almost as if Google Drawings knows you want to make a flowchart.

Moving items backward / forward.

Sometimes you'll want to write your processes down before you make the shapes that contain them. Unfortunately, this can create a problem when the shape sits on top of your text.

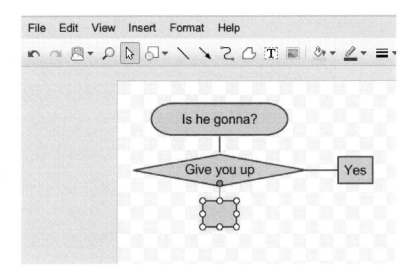

To get out of this sticky situation, click on the shape, go to format --> order --> send backward. Google Drawings, like a lot of other graphic editors, uses layers. The "send backward" command moves the shape one layer back, which in this case, places the text on top of it.

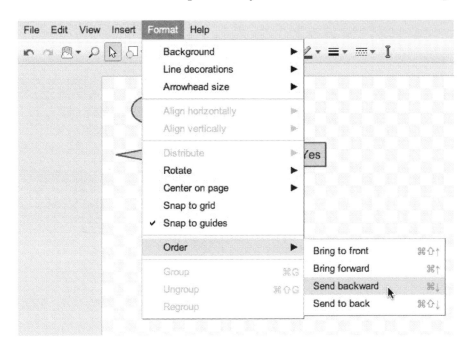

Pay attention to the keyboard shortcuts next to each command. If you're using these commands all the time, you'll save yourself a few steps.

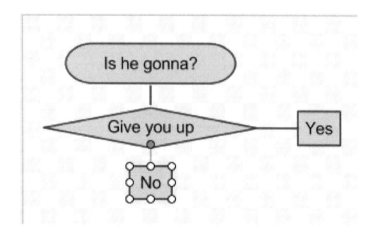

I highly encourage you to avoid reinventing the wheel when you're making flowcharts. If one part of your flowchart repeats itself, just copy and paste that section. This happens to be the case with the Rick Astley flowchart, pictured below.

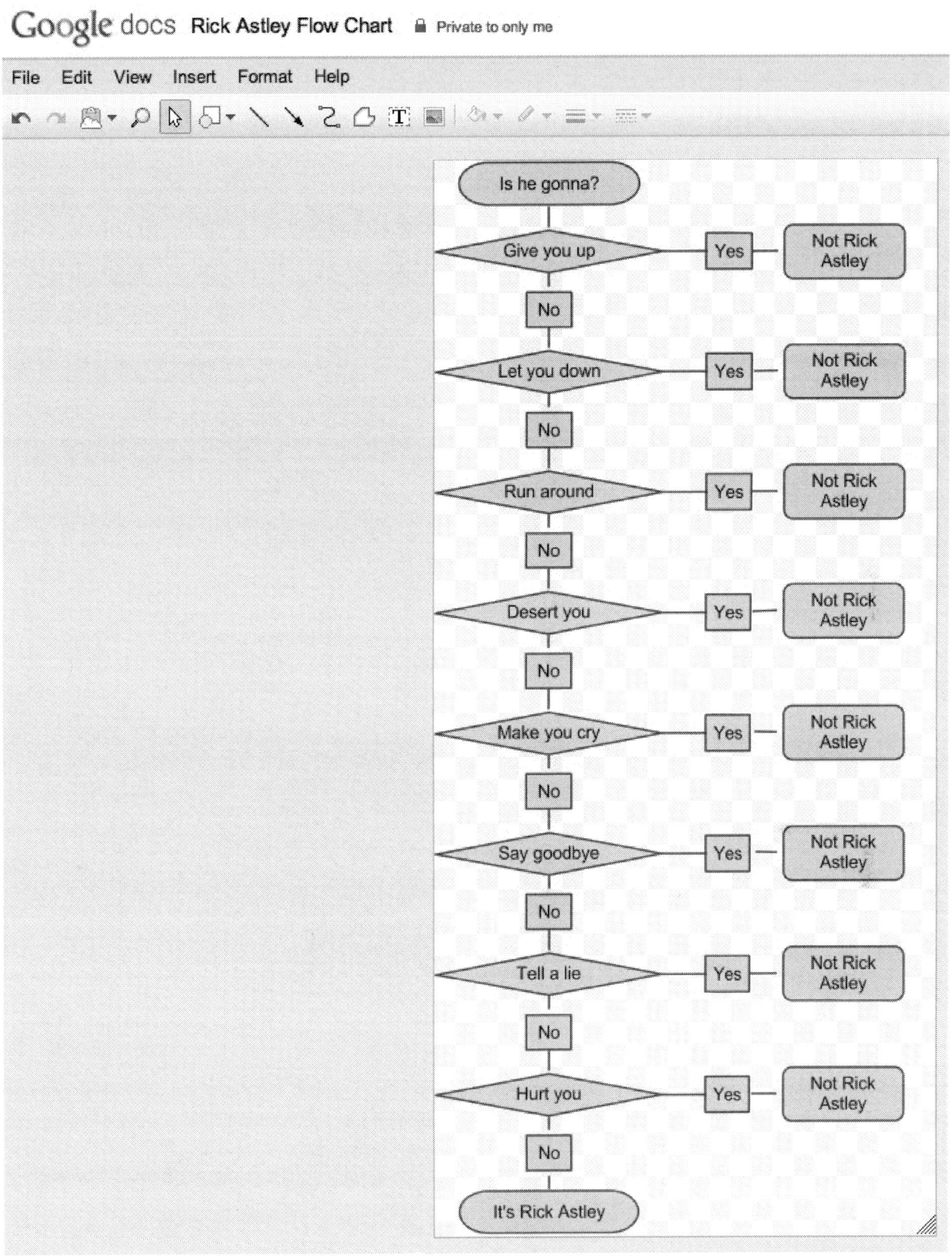

Google docs   Rick Astley Flow Chart   🔒 Private to only me

File   Edit   View   Insert   Format   Help

Is he gonna?

Give you up — Yes — Not Rick Astley

No

Let you down — Yes — Not Rick Astley

No

Run around — Yes — Not Rick Astley

No

Desert you — Yes — Not Rick Astley

No

Make you cry — Yes — Not Rick Astley

No

Say goodbye — Yes — Not Rick Astley

No

Tell a lie — Yes — Not Rick Astley

No

Hurt you — Yes — Not Rick Astley

No

It's Rick Astley

Saving your Google Drawings.

Now that we've got our Rick Astley flow chart, we can do a bunch of different things with it. Aside from copying our drawing to the web clipboard and pasting it into a presentation or Google Doc, we can download it as a PDF, PNG, JPG, or SVG file. Just go to file --> download as, and pick your preferred file type.

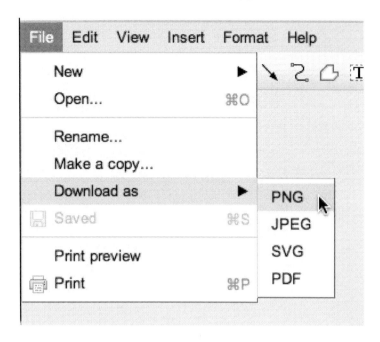

Here's our flow chart in PDF format. Before you print, you need to download your graphic to one of the four file formats.

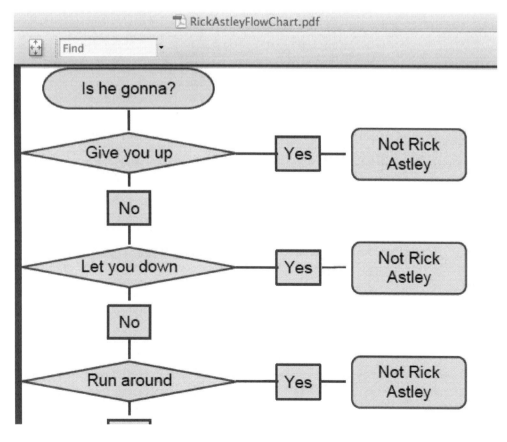

From here, you can print your drawing like you would if you were using Adobe Photoshop or any other illustration software.

Playing around with Google Drawings' other tools.

Google Drawings has a bunch of other tools for the aspiring artist. You can create curvy objects, arcs, squiggles, and nearly anything else you can think of. Here's a short overview.

We'll start off with the curve tool. I like using this one to make bobbly head shapes with weak facial features. You can find this tool by going to insert --> curve or by clicking on the icon to the right of the arrow tool.

When you use the curve tool, you start out with a single straight line. As you click to add more waypoints, the line curves around the points until you finally close off the shape.

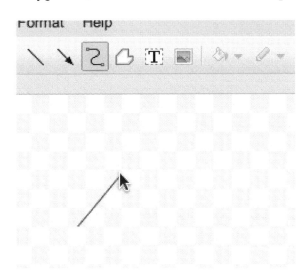

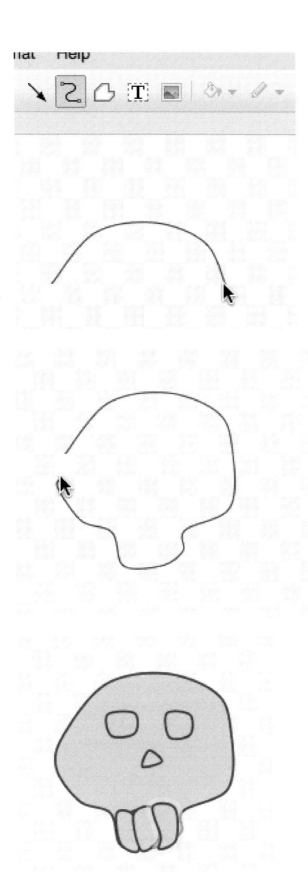

When you're finished drawing your shape, it gets filled in with the fill color. If you want to change the fill color, just click on the paint bucket icon to the right of the picture icon.

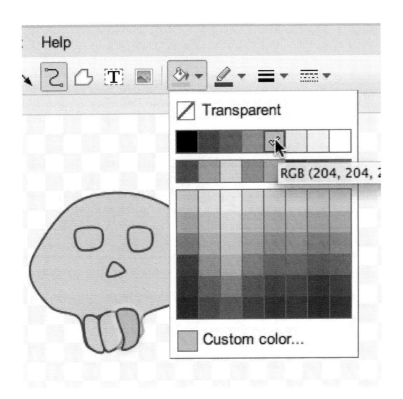

You can also change the line color and thickness with the tools to the right of the paint bucket. Here, I've increased the thickness of the tooth outline.

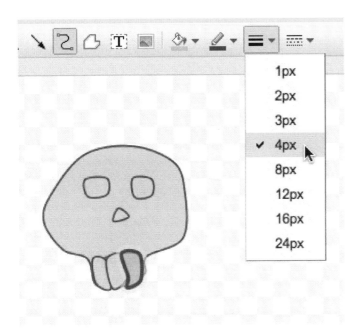

With Google Drawings, it's really easy to go back to any shape you've created and make changes to the line width, fill color, etc. Just go to the pointer tool, click on the shape, and make the change.

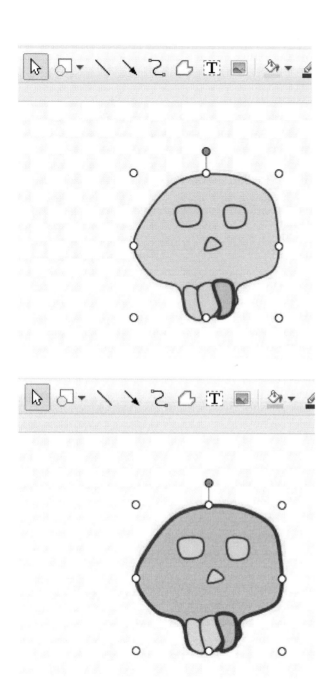

And voila, the final piece.

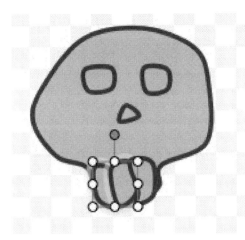

Try out the polygonal shape tool. It's right next door.

The polygonal shape tool works just like the curve tool, but it doesn't round the corners. It's great for anything that requires a hard edge like, say, a robot. You can find the polygonal shape tool to the right of the curve tool.

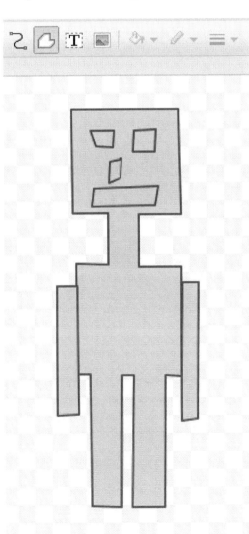

When you use the polygonal shape tool in conjunction with the curve tool, you can come up with just about any shape imaginable.

Make an arc with the arc tool.

The arc tool can come in handy when you least expect it. An arc is basically a section of a circle, and that's exactly what the arc tool makes. To find the arc tool, go to insert --> arc from the top menu.

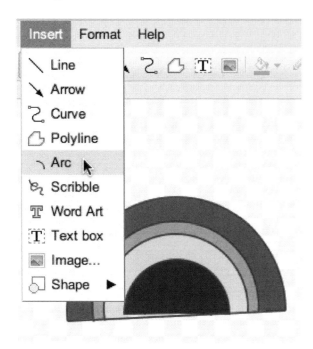

To start using the arc tool, you need to hold down the mouse button and drag to create a line that will represent the radius of your arc. For those of you who don't remember trigonometry, the radius is the distance from the center of a circle to its outside edge. The arc tool draws an arc around the radius you give it. Remember this as you make your line.

You may have already guessed that we're going to use the arc tool to draw a rainbow. We'll start with a small arc, and then we'll expand upon it as we go.

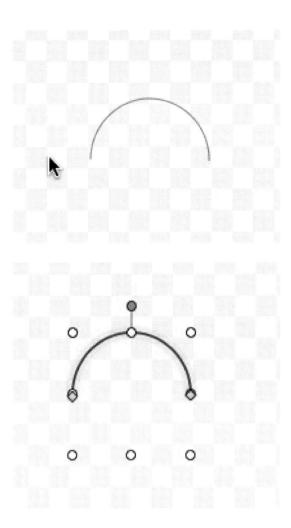

Once we've made our first arc, we don't need to keep making arcs. It's better to copy it, paste it, and do some resizing on the new one.

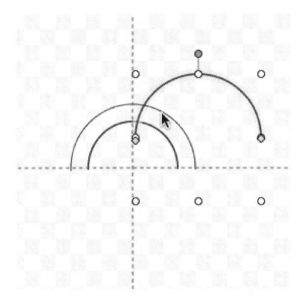

Notice how the two arcs line up with the crosshairs. Keep taking advantage of this as you create more complex shapes out of simple ones.

A few more copy and paste jobs, and we're done with this phase.

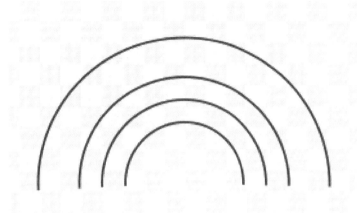

To get the colors, we need only select the arc and pick a color with the paint bucket. Let's start with the outer edge moving inward. We have to do that because the outside arc is "on top" of all the other arcs. After we change the color, we need to move the arc to the back of all the other shapes so its fill color doesn't cover up all the other arcs.

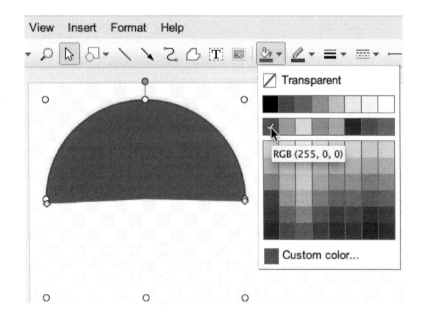

Our red arc is sitting on top of all the other arcs. Let's move it back. Go to format --> order --> send to back.

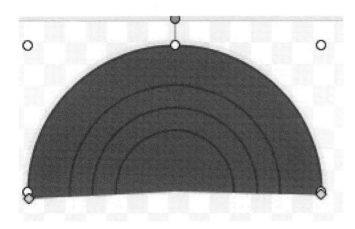

Ah, much better. Now that the outside arc is in the back, we can click on the inner arc, give it a color, and send it one layer back (but not all the way to the back or else the red arc will sit on top of it). The command for that is format --> order --> send backward.

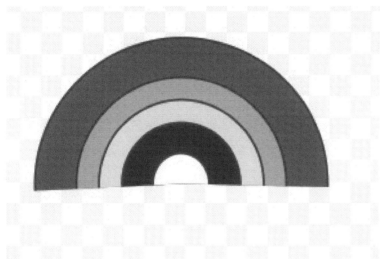

Keep coloring the arcs and sending them backward until you get to the final arc, which you will give a white color. And that's how you make a rainbow with Google Drawings.

One word of caution. I sometimes lose track of my shapes and have to move them around to find them. If you need to break your rainbow apart to find some of the arcs hidden beneath it, remember that you can easily put it all back together with the red dashed alignment crosshairs.

Mentioning some of the other tools.

I haven't covered all of the tools in Google Drawings because some of them aren't particularly remarkable. The scribble tool is kind of fun to play with, but honestly, it isn't all that useful for someone who's doing real work. You basically hold down the mouse button and draw like you would with a pen. When you're done, Google Drawings will give a slight curve to what you've drawn so it looks like handwriting.

And then there's the Word Art tool. Again, not that remarkable. It's just a more stylized version of the text tool. It creates text that acts more like a shape, so you can give it a fill color, rotate it, and do most of the things you would do with shapes. Give it a try if you're going to make a birthday party advertisement or a "lost dog" poster.

Well, we've certainly come a long way since you began with Google Drawings. Now you know how to create flow charts and work with the different drawing tools so your presentations have a little more pizzazz. And because you're doing all of your work online, there's absolutely no chance you'll ever lose it. Just sign into your Google Docs account, and it will always be there, even when your idiot roommate opens your window and forgets to shut it as a thunderstorm rolls through your hometown, exposing your laptop to a torrential downpour. You know, the kinds of things that never happen to people like you.

Conclusion

Now that you've mastered Google Docs, a whole cloud-based world awaits you. More and more professionals are moving their work over to Google Docs because it provides extra security, it's more conducive to collaboration, and did we mention *it's free?* Even if you decide you don't want to do most of your work on Google Docs, at the very least, don't give Microsoft or Apple any more of your money for software that should be free by now.

And if you really dig the cloud, there are an increasing number of applications moving to it every day. It won't be long before you no longer have to edit videos, photos, or anything else on your desktop. It will all be done online, and it will be faster.

It's good to embrace services like Google Docs. If enough people find them to be useful, software companies will have no choice but to put more of their software online for public use. Could you imagine a world in which you had to pay $100 to use Facebook every time you upgrade to a new computer? It sounds absurd, but that's the current predicament we're facing with office software. It's time to take a stand.

We hope you enjoyed this guide, and more importantly, we hope you found it useful. Google Docs has become a staple in our office, and we hope it'll do the same for you. Best of luck with all of your future projects!

Chapter 11: Google Picasa

Introduction

Picasa and Picasa Web Albums are image editing and sharing services from Google. Owned by Google since 2004, the Picasa's name is both a nod to the Spanish painter Pablo Picasso, and a combination of the words 'pic' (picture) and 'casa' (house).

Unlike Flickr and Photobucket, Picasa's functionality is not limited to online storage and sharing. Picasa Web Albums seamlessly integrates with Picasa, a software program for editing and organizing photos on your computer.

Once installed, Picasa automatically locates all images on your computer and organizes them. Picasa also utilizes facial recognition software that can organize photos based on the people in them. Picasa is available for PC, Mac, and Linux. Picasa syncs directly to the web through Picasa Web Albums. Once you have uploaded an album, if you add or remove photos or edit an image, simply select the 'sync to web' button to update your online album.

Basic Features

How do I join Picasa?

Anyone can download Picasa editing software for their computer. Go to http://picasa.google.com/ and select the 'download Picasa' button. You will then be prompted to sign in with a Google account. To use Picasa Web Albums, you will also need a Google account. If you do not already have a Google account, you can create one (for free) at https://www.google.com/accounts/NewAccount.

Picasa software is free. Picasa Web Albums is also free, although free photo storage is limited to 1 GB. If you need additional storage, you will have to pay, based on tiered system. For example, 20 GB is $5 per year, while 1 TB is $256 per year. This storage is shared across all Google products, including Gmail and Google Docs.

What is the difference between Picasa and Picasa Web Albums?

Picasa is free photo editing and organizing software that runs off your computer. Picasa Web Albums is an online photo sharing site. While the two programs can be used separately, they seamlessly integrate, making editing and uploading photos as simple as a few mouse clicks.

What are the main features of Picasa?

Picasa allows you to organize and edit photos directly on your computer. The left column displays a list of all the folders containing photos on your computer. A green arrow indicates the photo has been uploaded to Picasa Web Albums, and circular blue arrows indicate the 'sync' feature is activated for the folder. The bottom of Picasa is the 'Photo Tray,' a workstation for photos with quick links for editing, blogging, printing, and ordering pictures. The main section where you view photos is called the 'Lightbox.'

Folders:

Lightbox:

Photo Tray:

How do I organize my photos in Picasa?

When you install Picasa, the software will automatically search and organize all your existing photos.

Depending on the amount of data on your computer, this process can take anywhere from a few minutes to an hour. When the scan is complete, Picasa will list all the images on your computer. By default, this list is sorted by creation date, but you can change this by selecting 'View,' then 'Folder View,' and 'Sort by Name.' You may wish to rename or resort your photos. You can use Picasa to rename an entire group of photos at once. First, select the folder where the photos are located. Use the shift key to select multiple photos at once from the Lightbox. Select 'File' and then 'Rename.' You can also drag and drop photos from one folder to another.

How do I edit my photos?

Open Picasa and double click the picture you wish to edit to open the editing screen. The editing menu contains three tabs, 'Basic Features', 'Tuning', and 'Effects.' 'Basic Features' includes an 'I'm Feeling Lucky' button that will automatically balance color and contrast in your photo. You can also manually adjust color and contrast from the 'Tuning' tab. While these adjustments are not as precise as Photoshop, they provide quality improvements for the majority of your photos. If you don't like an adjustment, simply click the 'undo' button to undo the previous edit.

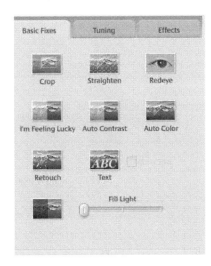

When you edit your photos, Picasa does not alter the original image. If you save the edits you make, Picasa will create a new version of the image, preserving the original.

What are the main features of Picasa Web Albums?

Picasa Web Albums allow you to share your photos with friends, family and the Picasa web community. Quick links from the right menu bar allow you to tag images, identify people in your photos, add locations, share albums and photos, and manage privacy.

top menu:

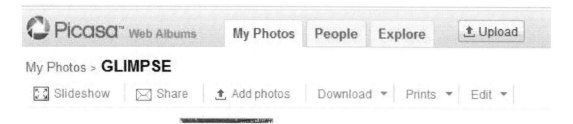

right menu bar:

What is the 'My Photos' tab?

The photos tab shows all your albums organized by privacy, depending on whether they are public or unlisted.

What is the 'People' tab?

The people tab keeps track of all the people in your photos. Picasa's software automatically recognizes faces. Once you label these faces -- and sync your labels with your online albums -- the people page will show all the people in your photos. You can label and identify faces through the People tab.

What is the 'Explore' tab?

The explore feature allows you to browse public photos. You can also explore images based on popular tags and locations.

What information is on the right menu?

The right menu contains a link to your profile and album or photo information, depending on which you are currently viewing. If you are viewing a photo, you will see information about when the photo was taken and the size of the image. You can edit and add information using the links in this menu.

How do I upload photos to Picasa Web Albums?

You can upload to Picasa Web Albums through Picasa. Select your album, and then select the 'sync to web' feature from the top right hand corner. You can also upload your album by selecting the 'Upload' button from the Photo Tray. If you are not using Picasa, you can still add images to Picasa Web Albums by using the 'Upload' button to directly upload images from your hard drive.

How do I share my photos in Picasa and Picasa Web Albums?

In Picasa, there are two main ways to share your photos: uploading the image to the web or emailing the image. The Upload and Email buttons are located in the Photo Tray. In Picasa Web Albums, you can share your photos by emailing friends and family a link to an individual image or an entire album. Selecting the 'share' button will open an email screen for you to send an email link through your Gmail account. You can also grab the link yourself by clicking on the 'link to this Album' button on the right menu or the 'link to this Photo' from the photo page. This menu also contains buttons to post your photo to Google Buzz, Blogger or Twitter.

How do I print photos?

You can print photos from either Picasa or Picasa Web Albums. To print from Picasa, select the 'Print' or 'Shop' buttons from the Photo Tray menu. To print from Picasa Web Albums, select the 'Prints' button under the 'My Photos' tab.

Advanced Features

How do I manage privacy settings?

Picasa Web Albums has three levels of album visibility: 'Public on the web,' 'Anyone with the link,' and 'Private.' If you select 'Public on the web,' your images may appear in public searches. If you select 'Anyone with a link,' only people who receive your unique authorization key (a randomly generated combination of letters and numbers) will be able to view these photos. This authorization key is included in the url to your album or photo. With the 'Private' setting, you specify the exact users who have access to your photos. These individuals must verify their identity by signing into their Google Accounts. Failure to do so will prevent them from viewing your photos.

You can manage access privileges by selecting the '**Share**' button in Picasa or Picasa Web Albums. You can share with individual people by adding email addresses or share with an entire Google contact group. In Picasa, click the 'Plus People' button to add a Google contact group; in Picasa Web Albums, select the boxes next to each contact group. If you change your mind about sharing, you can remove an individual or contact group at any time by deselecting the individual or group.

Can I sync multiple folders at once?

'Sync to web' is a feature the updates your Picasa Web Albums to reflect any edits or additions you have made to your folders in Picasa. 'Batch upload' is a tool that allows you to sync multiple albums at once. Select 'tools' from the main menu and then click 'batch upload.' This will generate a list of your albums. Select the ones you wish to update and upload, and click okay.

How do I add tags, people and captions in Picasa Web Albums?

To add tags or people, first select the photo you wish to tag. Then select the 'tag' or 'people' links from the right menu. A red box with orange endpoints will appear in the center of your photo. Move the box to the desired location and then enter the tag name or person in the dialogue box below. To add a caption, click on the blue 'Add a Caption' text below the photo and enter the desired caption.

Add a Caption

What is the Geo-Tag feature?

The Geo-Tag feature, accessible in Picasa from Photo Tray or the right menu in Picasa Web Albums, adds your images to Google Earth. In order to use the Geo-Tag feature in Picasa, you must install Google Earth on your computer. You can also tag photos uploaded to Picasa Web Albums. Once your image is uploaded, click 'Add location' and type in the country, city or address, depending on how specific you would like to be. Saving this location will add your image to the Google Earth map.

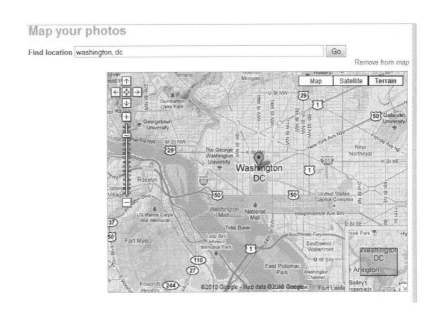

How do I add content to my blog or website from Picasa? How is this different from Picasa Web Albums?

In Picasa, you can publish albums and photos directly to your blog or website by highlighting a photo and then clicking the 'Blog This' button in the Photo Tray. From Picasa Web Albums, select the 'Link to this Album' or 'Link to the Photo' button from the right menu and copy the link to embed the image.

How do I make a slideshow?

To make a slideshow in Picasas Web Albums, click 'Link to this Album' and then select the 'Embed slide show' option. Selecting this feature will open a new dialogue box where you can customize a portable slideshow for your website or blog. Select a size and whether you want to include existing photo captions. Picasa Web Albums will automatically generate code to copy and paste onto your site.

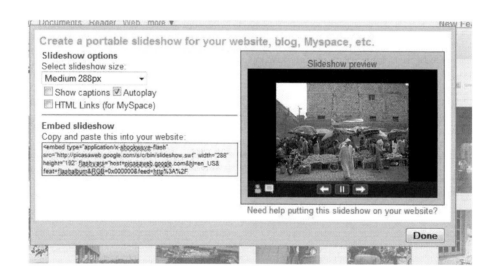

What is the collage button?

The collage button arranges photos from an album in an interesting pattern, such as a mosaic, tile, picture pile, grid or contact sheet. This button is located in the Picasa Photo Tray.

picture pile collage:

contact sheet collage:

What is the star button?

The star button is a handy tool for tagging your favorite photos. For example, as you organize photos on your computer, you may find you've got 378 photos from the holidays last year, but only 10 really good ones. Star these 10 photos by selecting a photo and clicking the gold star button from the Workstation. Now you can instantly access these favorites in the future without scrolling through all 378 photos again.

What special effects can I add to my photos?

Picasa offers a variety of special effects under the 'Effects' tab. With the single click of a button, you can alter an image.

Original image:

Sepia image:

Tinted image:

Can I retouch my photos?

Yes, Picasa includes a basic retouch feature. While this feature is not as advanced as Photoshop, you can retouch photo imperfections and blemishes. Zoom in on the area in need of retouching, adjust the retouch brush to the appropriate size and click on the spot to correct. You will need to do this several times over the area to ensure a natural look.

Is there a fast way to search for photos in Picasa?

Yes! The top right menu bar includes a 'search' box. Type the name of a folder or photo and only contents matching this name will appear.

About Minute Help

Minute Help Press is building a library of books for people with only minutes to spare. Follow @minutehelp on Twitter to receive the latest information about free and paid publications from Minute Help Press, or visit minutehelpguides.com.

Made in the USA
Lexington, KY
09 December 2014